More Nuggets of Writing Gold

By
Leeann Betts and Donna Schlachter

ISBN: 978-1-943688-45-6
(c) 2018

Cover design by Donna Schlachter

Published by PLS Bookworks, Denver, Colorado

Check our website for upcoming releases:
www.PLSBookworks.com

FOREWORD

It seems many authors enjoyed the first volume of *Nuggets of Writing Gold*, and asked for more.

So here it is. If you haven't read the first book, you might think of picking it up. Formatted similarly to this one, with different articles, essays, exercises, and helps, you'll find a well-rounded introduction to the writing life, as well as discussion of topics such as the passion to write, the writing journey, the craft of writing, research, and much more. Some articles don't contain separate exercises because the majority of the article was a list of actions to incorporate into your writing life.

Constructed to not only lead you through a particular topic, but also to provide opportunity to practice what you just learned, this book will prove to be a tool you'll want to refer to time and again.

For those who lead writer's groups or critique groups, you might want to choose one of the essays as a discussion and practical writing topic for meetings.

However you use this book, we pray it's a blessing to you and the call to write in your life.

You might notice there's a lot more of God mentioned in this book. I think that's because there's a lot more of God in our lives now, and we unashamedly point people to Him. That doesn't negate the wisdom and practicality of the articles and exercises.

Leeann Betts and Donna Schlachter

www.LeeannBetts.com
www.DonnaSchlachter.com

Other Books By Leeann Betts:
Counting the Days: a 31-day devotional
In Search of Christmas Past – a novel
Available at Amazon.com in print & digital, & at Smashwords.com in digital

By the Numbers series featuring Carly Turnquist, forensic accountant
No Accounting for Murder
There Was a Crooked Man
Unbalanced
Five and Twenty Blackbirds
Broke, Busted, and Disgusted
Hidden Assets
Petty Cash
Available at Amazon.com in print & digital, & at Smashwords.com in digital

By Leeann and Donna:
Nuggets of Writing Gold -- articles and essays on writing.
Available at Amazon.com in print & digital, & at Smashwords.com in digital

Books by Donna Schlachter:
Second Chances and Second Cups, A short story collection.
The Physics of Love: where the past, the present, and the future collide
The Mystery of Christmas Inn, Colorado
Christmas Under the Stars
Transformation – a devotional releasing Jan 2018

Mended by God series
Broken Dreams, Mended Heart
Broken Dreams, Mended Family
Broken Dreams, Mended Marriage
Available at Amazon.com in print & digital, & at Smashwords.com in digital

From Barbour Publishing:
Echoes of the Heart -- The Pony Express Romance Collection
A Prickly Affair -- Bouquet of Brides Romance Collection
Train Ride to Heartbreak -- Mail Order Brides Romance Collection
Detours of the Heart – MISSAdventure Brides, releasing 2019

Follow us:
Donna: www.HiStoryThruTheAges.wordpress.com
Leeann: www.AllBettsAreOff.wordpress.com
We are also active on Facebook and Twitter

Sign up for our free quarterly newsletter and receive a free book:
Donna (historical) www.HiStoryThruTheAges.com
Leeann (contemporary) www.LeeannBetts.com

Contents

Idea Generation 7
   A Change is as Good as a Rest 8
   Coffee Shop Inspiration 10
   Donna's 10 favorite places to do research: 12
   Embarrassing Moments that Make Good Reading 14
   Finding Inspiration in the Strangest Places 16
   Generating Blog Post Ideas 18
   The Perfect Road Trip 20
Planning the Story 23
   Writing What You Don't Know 24
   A Book Fit for The King 26
   A New Reality -- From a memory to a memoir 28
   Choosing a Setting 30
   Defining Historical Fiction 32
   Fact or Fiction — Choosing Your Setting 34
   Interviewing Your Characters 36
   Memories and Memoirs 39
   People Just Like Me—and You 40
   Research Isn't Work 42
   Setting the Tone for a Series 44
   The Lies We Believe 47
   The Therapy Couch 50
   What's in a Name? 52
   Write What You Know 54
   Write What You Want to Know 56
   Writing A Novella 58
   Writing a Series 60
Writing the Story 61
   Cutting Extra Words 62
   The Action/Danger Hook 64
   The Opening Line 66
   Wrapping a Not-So-Unique Story in a Unique Setting 68
   Writing Your Family Story 70
Story Structure 73
   Create Questions in the Reader's Mind 74
   Entice Your Readers 76
   Dialogue techniques 78
   Romantic Tension 81
The Writing Life 83
   Creating a Pseudonym 84
   Credibility in our Lives and in our Writing 86
   Ghostwriting by any other name 88
   Ghostwriting isn't a mystery 90

- Holding it all together 92
- Hosting a Successful Book Event 95
- Judging a Writing Contest 98
- Online Courses 100
- These are a Few of my Favorite Things 102
- Rejection and Reality 104
- Unlocking the Doors 106
- Why Guest Blog? 108
- Self-Imposed Deadlines 110
- Writing Contest Do's and Don'ts 112
- Writing on a Deadline 115
- Writing Through the Summer –or any season 117
- Split Personality or Writing Under a Pen Name 119
- The 10-day Writing Challenge 121

Encouragement 123
- Hard Tack and Hard Knocks 124
- Hazy But Not Lazy Days 126
- Keep on Keeping on 128
- Knowing the Author 130
- No More Name-Dropping 132
- Numbers Don't Change 134
- One Mouthful at a Time 136
- The Call to Write 138
- Am I Invisible? 140
- Touched by an Angel 142

Subplots that won't sink your story – mini-conference 145

Resources 156

About the Author (s) 159

Idea Generation

A Change is as Good as a Rest

"A change is as good as a rest". My father used to say that a lot.

Lately I've been really tired. I thought I needed a rest. A vacation. And so I told some friends, "I'd like to take a vacation where I don't have to travel every day. Where I get to sleep in the same comfy bed every night. Where I don't have to cook, or clean, or make the bed."

The next day I learned that my attendance at a set of weekend meetings wasn't required. But I'd already booked the time off, reserved a hotel, and bought tickets to a museum in the area.

What to do?

Wait a minute. I was just saying I needed a vacation. Yippee!

Suddenly I was re-energized. I buckled down and accomplished a lot in one day. Caught up on my correspondence, cleaned out my email inbox, wrote some blogs that were due, and generally felt a lot better about myself, my schedule, and my workload.

Do you need a rest? Maybe all you really need is a "change". And while I wish I'd said I'd like to spend my vacation somewhere warm, like on a beach, I'll take what I've been given.

So if you need to make a "change", my first suggestion would be: be specific. There is nothing wrong with spelling out exactly what you want. Maybe a new car. Well, describe it. Perhaps you need a new house. Write down how many bedrooms, how many levels, even the color if you know it. Maybe lose weight. Decide what your ideal weight goal is.

Next, decide what the first step is to achieve your goal. If you want a new car, perhaps you need to start saving. A new house? Go to open houses in the area you'd like to live in. Lose weight? Decide what foods tempt you and get them out of the house.

Third step would be to visualize your change. Find pictures of that new car or new house. Post pictures of outfits you'd like to wear or the cruise ship you'll sail on when you can fit into a sleeker swimsuit.

Finally, do whatever it takes to achieve your goal. Need to save more money faster? What can you sell? What service can you cancel? Maybe you don't need a landline telephone and a cell phone. Maybe you can live without cable for a while. Don't want flabby skin after you reach your weight loss goal? Maybe you can walk some each day. Get up early and do some stretches. Join a gym.

Whatever your "change" is, you won't achieve it if you don't start. So start dreaming today, and tomorrow, put some action behind your dreams.

Takeaway: In order to write deep stories that will draw readers in, we need to be in prime emotional condition. We can't do that if we don't take care of ourselves.

Exercises:
1. If you're feeling physically exhausted, could there be a physical reason? What you're eating? Not getting enough sleep? What changes are you willing to make to improve how you feel?
2. If you're feeling emotionally exhausted, check your calendar. Schedule in some down time, some couple time, some family time.
3. How's your prayer life? If you aren't spending time with God now on a daily basis, perhaps now is the time to start. Get a Bible and a reading plan, and follow it. Spending time in the Word on a daily basis rejuvenates like nothing else.

Coffee Shop Inspiration

I'm sitting in a coffee shop trying to figure out what to write about this month. All around me are people sipping java or tea, munching bagels, meeting friends, talking on phones—and it hits me.

I am looking in at the goldfish bowl.

For example, already today I eavesdropped on three friends who meet every two months to discuss a book, like a mini book club. While I couldn't see the title of the one they are reading, it seemed to be full of witticisms, observations, and helpful insights. For example, one was about Solomon, the wisest man who ever lived. He married 1,000 women, which were his downfall. So if a man doesn't marry 1,000 women, he'll already be smarter than the wisest man who ever lived.

Later there was a table of older women gathering tables from near and far, even settling for round tables, to get enough seating for their group of about 20 women. Along comes one woman with a little girl, maybe about 4 or so. And I got to wondering if this older woman was the grandmother—or the mother. And plot ideas sprang forth immediately.

A few days ago, at a table nearby, sat a middle eastern man and two women. Sometimes they spoke in English, sometimes in another language that sounded Arabic. Sometimes they mixed their sentences together, using English words in the middle of a sentence with this other language. For example, I heard the word 'embassy' and 'must be careful' in the midst of other words I couldn't understand. Got me thinking about a suspense plot.

Every Monday when I am here, there is a woman sitting nearby who is a counselor of some kind. I've heard her talking to a client on the phone about an issue the client was going through. Not details, but I saw this counselor's demeanor change from the way she looked when she was typing on her laptop—doing right-brain work—to the way her face softened and her posture relaxed as she talked to her client—left-brain work. She'd make a good character where I could show both sides of her at work.

Right now there is a couple sitting next to me who are speaking Chinese, perhaps. I don't understand a word they are saying, but they've been very animated at times, voices raised, hand gestures, smiles. Are they planning a business move? To buy a house? Get a cat? Have another child in contravention of China's one-child law? What if one of the couple wants to return to China, but the other doesn't? Will that impact their decision?

Sitting in a coffee shop may sound like a waste of time. Usually I come here just to get away from the laundry or to meet fellow writers. But perhaps I need this unique stimulation to get the old grey cells, as Hercule Poirot would say, working.

Takeaway: Sometimes changing our surroundings gets us looking at characters differently.

Exercises:
1. Go to a coffee shop and eavesdrop on conversations around you. Can you use some of what you hear?
2. Hang around a central bus depot or train station. Watch the people; make notes of what they do.
3. Go to the airport and hang around the main concourse. Make up stories about the people you see.

Donna's 10 favorite places to do research:

    1.   Your local library: most libraries have a local history section or a genealogy section, and in larger towns and cities, you will likely also find newspaper archives. Look for books written during the time period you're writing about.
    2.   Historical societies: often have diaries and journals of residents, albums of pictures, and lots of newspaper and magazine clippings. Most do a calendar each year as a fund raiser, so ask for back copies that are probably reduced in price now.
    3.   Historical markers: most states have dozens of historical markers along the highways. Don't be afraid to get off the highway for a few miles and follow a rutted trail into the middle of a huge meadow to discover a single marker about an obscure Civil War Battle that few have heard of.
    4.   Trail Interpretation Centers: not only do they talk about the trail but usually they include history of the local area as well.
    5.   Visitor Centers: often the people who work or volunteer at these centers are locals who know the local history or have an interest in a special piece of history.
    6.   State Park centers and gift shops: the people who work here usually know a lot about the area, or know the people in the area who know a lot.
    7.   Museums: there are museums for just about every interest. I have visited airplane and glider museums; Pony Express museums; Old Western Town museums; War museums; aircraft carrier museum; police and military museum; firearms museums; stagecoach museum; carriage museum; and automobile museums.
    8.   History Museums: particularly in larger cities, these museums bring in and rotate through a variety of exhibits during the year. Become a member and get on their mailing list to stay up to date. For example, Denver recently had the Sherlock Holmes exhibit and the Poison exhibit.
    9.   Entertainment attractions: for example, in Las Vegas, there are virtual reality-type shows where you can be a CSI and walk through a crime scene, look at evidence, and enter a report as to your findings.

10. Movies: I like to watch movies set in the time period I'm currently writing in. The closer the movie was made to the event the better, I've found.

Takeaway: Go to a quality source for your information.

Exercises:
1. When you use the internet, check at least 5 different sites, and get the same information from at least 2 different sources. Otherwise, you could be using faulty information.
2. Personal sources, such as interviews, diaries, journals, and original source documents are best.
3. Confirm newspaper accounts, since reporters don't always get the story right.

Embarrassing Moments that Make Good Reading

I love the coffee mug that says, "Be nice to me, or I will put you in my next book."

But I think an even better one would be, "Wanted: fools that make characters of themselves."

Because we all have those moments we hope nobody else saw.

Which are priceless tidbits for our stories.

You know what I'm talking about. Those things that nobody would believe.

Except they really happened.

Like the time I walked through the halls of my middle school with my uniform skirt up around my backside as my entire eighth grade class watched.

A dog had wandered into the classroom, and I'd scooped him up and marched him to the door where I released him.

Took me about three years to live that one down.

Or the time I was singing along to a Christian song on my Walkman as I took my daily walk. At the top of my lungs. Then I stopped to tie my shoelace and discovered two boys walking behind me who'd heard every off-key word. Because I can't carry a tune in a bucket.

Then there was the time when I was about four and a neighbor boy took my bicycle. I asked my dad to get my bike back, but he said I needed to do it for myself. So I marched down there, pushed the boy off, and got my bike back. Then the boy ran to his father who came to complain about me being a bully.

Embarrassing, yes, but great fodder for your stories.

So the next time something happens to you or somebody else, consider how you might write that into a story, or even into a character's backstory. Knowing my character went through this bicycle incident reveals to me their profound sense of justice, their desire for all to be right with their world, and the courage to be the change they want to see.

Takeaway: Keep a notebook with you at all times or make notes on your smartphone of funny or embarrassing things you see each day.

Exercises:
1. Write out the story of an embarrassing moment from your childhood.
2. Write out the story of an embarrassing moment that happened to someone else.
3. How can you use these in your current story, even if you have to change some details because of genre, setting, or period?

Finding Inspiration in the Strangest Places

Sometimes life is just plain hard. Hard to understand. Hard to bear. Hard to believe.

It's in those times, when I think there is no getting through, scrambling over, or finding my way around a situation that God speaks to me in the strangest of places.

For example, recently I purchased an old 1920's typewriter, sight unseen, with visions of using it at a book launch. When the machine was delivered, I was aghast at how OLD it was! Somehow I'd expected it to look like those ones you see on eBay where they want $500. But I'd only paid $30.

It wasn't shiny—it was rusty.

It didn't work—every key was glued into place with almost 100 years of dust, dirt, leaves, cobwebs—I even found a few spider carcasses.

Ugh! Yuck!

But I tackled the project to restore it to at least working condition. I watched videos on YouTube, and was once again reminded that people are more likely to watch a video than click on a link and that I needed to make some videos and do a book trailer for each of my books.

As I took the machine apart, I carefully separated the screws into different containers so I'd know which ones went where, and I got an idea for an article about organizing my historical research bits and pieces of information.

Cleaning the parts, oiling them, and testing them reminded me of the scripture passage I'd been reading that morning—to run with endurance the race set before me.

Suddenly, quitting was not an option!

And finally, as I tested each key, tightened the last screw, and admired my completed work, I thought about the typewriter itself, wondering about the people who'd used it. "There must be a hundred stories in this typewriter," I thought. "Stories about where it's been. What was written on it. The business that owned it first. How excited, in 1920, the first user must have been. What disappointments did they face when the Depression hit? Was this used in some way for the war effort? Did an owner refuse to switch over to a newer model or was this stored in an attic when electric models came out?"

I had the basis for a book of short stories about this typewriter.

So you see, inspiration can come from anywhere. This typewriter spurred me to commit to myself to do a book trailer, reminded me of scripture, encouraged me with an idea for an article and a book. And just looking at the typewriter will keep those things in mind.

Takeaway: When you feel like quitting, ask another 'what if?' question about your story.

Exercises:
1. Pull out an unfinished project and complete it for that special sense of accomplishment.
2. Pull out your idea file and write a short summary of the story.
3. Find an old family photo—preferably one where you don't know all the people in it—and choose one to be the main character in your next book. Then write a character sketch.

Generating Blog Post Ideas

For someone who never struggles to come up with a book idea, I sit at my computer every month as I prepare to pen blog posts, and I ask myself, "What do this blog's readers want to know?" and "What can I tell them about that?"

So today I googled that question: top blog posts for writers.

And now I'm going to share one blogger's response.

Molly Green has an entire article of 101 best blog posts which is, as you can imagine, full of information. Here are a few I think you might find interesting, but you really should check out the whole list:

1. The best blog posts you've read the past week or month – with links: That one is easy -- http://purposefulfaith.com/afraid-to-be-happy/

2. Writers (or authors, teachers, industry leaders, philanthropists) who inspire you – that was easy too. Ted Dekker sent a link to a great little ebook, and if you haven't read it, you should: should – https://thecreativeway.com/4-dm-sell-out-bonuses

3. Your favorite blogs. Example: Belinda Pollard's **4 useful blogs to get you started in self-publishing** – although I'd not heard of this author, I liked the article and subscribed to receive blogs by email.

There are nearly 100 more ideas in this particular article, and although I haven't checked out all of the following, here are some more examples:

http://www.webdesignrelief.com/40-blog-post-ideas-novelists-poets-creative-writers/

http://weblogs.about.com/od/startingablog/tp/BlogPostIdeas.htm

http://www.yourwriterplatform.com/blog-post-ideas-for-writers/

http://www.30daybooks.com/28-blog-post-ideas-for-writers-and-authors-to-use-today-with-some-fill-in-the-blank-titles/

If most of your subscribers are readers or you want to attract more readers to your blog:

http://startbloggingonline.com/101-blog-post-ideas-that-make-your-blog-hot/ -- this has actually been a goal of mine, so I'm going to check out the complete list

http://www.copyblogger.com/brainstorm-blog-topics/

http://theblogstylist.com/blog-post-ideas/

Takeaway: Ideas abound. We just need to know where to look for them.

Exercises:
1. Pick one or two of the blogs listed above and follow them daily for a week to see the kinds of things they blog about.
2. Sketch out a list of blog topics you could write credibly about.
3. Set up a blog schedule at a free service like SignUp Genius and invite your author friends to guest blog for you. You decide how often you want guest bloggers.

The Perfect Road Trip

I love road trips. I love planning road trips.
Because I use road trips for research.
Yes, even though I write contemporary suspense as well as historical romance/suspense, you might think I only need the research for the historical stuff, right?
Wrong.
Unless you are only going to write about one setting where you've lived all your life, you're going to need to do some research. And even if you create your own settings, like I tend to do, you still need to see what other places look like.
I'll give you some ideas from a story idea percolating in my brain: *in order to receive their inheritance, three sisters who haven't spoken to each other in more than ten years take a road trip to return their father's ashes to his hometown.* I even have a title: *Taking Daddy Home.*
Here's my process for a successful road trip:

1. Decide where the story will take place: In my novel, Daddy died in Portland, Oregon; grew up in Portland, Maine. See the irony of living and dying in cities with the same name but on opposite sides of the country?

2. How will you get from point A to point B? So, to research my story, I will need to drive it. Doesn't mean I have to do it all in one trip. Maybe your book takes place at one main location, such as a beach. Plan a trip to the specific beach, or tour a number of beaches and create a conglomerate of details to make up your own beach location.

3. What problems will you introduce, and how does this influence your road trip? Look for the perfect place to put your character in peril of some sort. In my story, I'll pick a secluded stretch of highway for them to have a flat tire, a small town where they don't feel welcome, a rundown motel along the interstate where they think they're seeing ghosts, and a biker bar where they get in the middle of a gang fight.

4. What do you want your characters to learn? Give them something to do besides just driving down the road watching the gas gauge. Create some conflict between what the characters want to do.

5. Location, location, location: I glean facts from places I've visited then combine them to create my settings. For example, my latest Carly Turnquist mystery, *Five and Twenty Blackbirds* is fashioned after the town my father and step-mother, who I loved, were married in, Cave Creek, AZ. If you use real places for your settings, you'll absolutely want to visit to get the street names and directions right.

6. Local history, traditions, legends: look for ways to incorporate the truth about your locations into your story, even if you're creating your own settings.

7. Record this information in useful ways: take pictures, use a digital voice recorder, and make written notes. Collect brochures and printed information. Ask questions at visitor centers and museums.

Now that you have the outline for a road trip and the tools to gather the information you need, get busy!

Takeaway: Research isn't only for history.

Exercises:
1. You can take a road trip and still be home tonight. Plan something that takes about two hours to get there; spend the day; return home tonight.
2. A long weekend is a perfect opportunity for a road trip. Take a look at your calendar and find a date soon.
3. A week or more makes a great road trip, too. Make plans for further afield. Check the weather, availability of local attractions and places to visit along the way. Plan for around 450 miles per day to give you time to stop and see something on the spur of the moment.

Planning the Story

Writing What You Don't Know

We've all heard that we should write about what we know. But what if you find out about a project that you don't know anything about but would like to learn?

I discovered since I started writing seriously that I love history. I met up with Mary Davis at an ACFW conference and asked her what she was working on. She said she and three other authors were putting together a proposal on the Pony Express. I said if there was an opening, I'd love to join.

I told my husband about this meeting, and he said, "Sounds like an excuse for a road trip." So I researched the Pony Express and learned that the only station in Colorado was in Julesburg. So we picked a long weekend and set out. Along the way, we stopped at the visitor center at Sterling, Colorado. I asked if they had information about the Pony Express, and she showed me the couple of pieces they had. She also said I should talk with the past president of the Colorado Pony Express Association. She called him, Gary came down, and we spent an hour talking about the Pony Express.

Prior to this trip, before I even knew if I'd be able to get in on Mary's collection, I'd visited the library and read a bunch of stuff about the Pony Express. I'd researched online, and I'd ordered a couple of books from Amazon.

A month later, Mary Davis emailed and said one of the ladies had to drop out and now there was an opening. Because I'd done the research, I was ready to submit a proposal.

What I've learned:

1. Writing only what I know boxes me in. Writing what I'd like to know allows me to learn and explore. I don't need to be an expert; I just need to know enough to sound credible. If I don't know a particular detail, I can always look it up online or find a book with the information.

2. Writers conferences are great places to connect with other authors as well as with agents and editors.

3. The more I learn about a subject, the more excited I get, and the easier it is to write about it.

4. No matter the topic, there is a book, a museum, or an expert out there.

5. Folks love talking about their jobs. Plan to interview someone.
6. Research the kind of museum you'd like to visit—many have virtual tours if you can't physically visit.

Takeaway: It's easier to write about a topic or place if you feel like you know something about it.

A Book Fit for The King

I wrote my dad's memoirs a couple of years ago. Because we don't live near each other, we spent time together at Christmas or Thanksgiving working on the book. I used a digital recorder and had a list of questions I needed answered. Once I got the story down, I'd send him several chapters at a time for him to review. Then I sent the final book, printed out in a binder, and he called with changes and corrections. Even once we sent it to a printer, we found errors in the galleys which we corrected.

My father held his book in his hand a month before he passed away.

He boasted to several people about his life story. The intake counselor at the hospice he went to was astounded he had a book, saying that many people came to this point in their lives wishing they'd written a book. She said she'd never known anybody who had.

I was so pleased to have been part of that process, to give my dad a book he was proud to hold in his hand. A book he was proud to have his name on.

Which got me to thinking about my other books. Would my Heavenly Father be proud to hold my other books in His hand? Would He be proud to have His Name on those books?

That changed the way I looked at my books. Because I realized they weren't mine at all. He is the author. I simply transcribe the stories for Him.

And as such, it's my job to be as accurate as I can. To show up for work every day. To do the best I can to listen and not inject myself into the story.

God's job is to create the stories. To communicate them to me. To correct me when I get off track.

I like the partnership I have with Him. It takes a lot of pressure off me. When I'm staring at the blank page, I simply pray, "Lord, thank You for letting me be the first person you've ever shown this story to. Help me hear You correctly and do the work of transcribing."

Knowing what I need to do and what I don't need to do makes the job a lot easier which means I'm having a lot more fun. I'm working on the next book in my dad's memoirs, and although he's with Jesus now, I hope he'd be just as proud to hold this book in his hand as he was with the first one.

And I pray God would be proud to have His name on every book I've written.

Takeaway: Writing a book God would be proud to have His name on doesn't mean we have to write scripture on every page and a salvation scene in every chapter. Telling stories that illustrate God's love for His children is one way to honor Him in our writing.

Exercises:
1. Read through a favorite Bible story and write a one-sentence summary of the story. Is this a story you'd like to set in a different time period? Maybe this should be your next project.
2. What kinds of stories get you excited to read or write? This could be a passion God has placed on your heart. Maybe this is your next project.
3. If you could write about anything, what would that be? How can you show God in the pages of the story, even if you never mention His name?

A New Reality -- From a memory to a memoir

Two years ago, my father called me with an interesting proposition: write his life store, keep all the profits, share the movie rights.

Now, right off the bat, he acknowledged that his story wasn't unique: a boy adopted by grandparents who didn't know his "sister" was really his mother until he was thirteen years old.

However, he felt the circumstances, the time period, and the setting would make the book unique. I thought it was high time somebody documented the events, since everybody involved was either really old or dead, and because I felt his family--my siblings--should know where we came from.

Over the next six months we met a couple of times. I recorded the time we spent discussing the book. He gave me contemporaneous documents in the form of cash books from his father's store and letters between his birth mother and his father. I researched what I could, got in touch with the town historian when necessary, and made up the rest.

That's right. A memoir, and I made stuff up.

Because the truth is, nobody knows everything that happened, or what was said, or even who was involved. So many times I asked my dad who was with him, and he couldn't remember everybody.

The first edits were interesting. I'd send it to him, and he'd send it back, "I don't think I said this" or "I don't think it happened like that". I'd ask, "Do you remember what did happen?" "No." "Then my version stands."

He finally came to terms with the fact that creative non-fiction is exactly that: creative.

We used the names of the original people, because this was going to be a family-only version. But he said he wanted the book published in the general market, so we agreed to change the names and a few other details so nobody knew for certain who was being talked about.

My dad held "his" book in his hands three weeks before he passed. He was as pleased as punch to see his name on the cover, to read his stories, his past.

And then he looked at me and said, "We need another book."

Except this time we didn't have two years. This time we had three weeks.

I wish I'd asked more questions. I pray he'd be as pleased to hold this new book in his hands. Once again, we published a family-only version first, and then the market version of the two books combined, *The Physics of Love*, released October 2016.

Hollywood, here we come!

Takeaway: Few people have a unique life story, but everybody has an interesting story.

Exercises:
1. Decide whose story you'd like to secure. Maybe start with an elderly friend or relative, or somebody whose health is poor. You won't have forever.
2. Get a digital recorder. If they feel more comfortable, leave it with them and tell them to just tell you their story.
3. If they're willing, make a list of interview questions that get basic details like date and place of birth, family history, any genealogy they know. Ask for photos and source documents.

Choosing a Setting

With so many great places to set a book, how do authors go about selecting that perfect location that is not merely a backdrop to the plot but actually becomes an integral character?

I go about this two ways: I either know the story and choose the setting based on what's going to happen in the story; or I know the location and want to set a good story there.

For example, in my first book, *No Accounting for Murder,* since I'm familiar with small East Coast towns (I lived in Newfoundland and Nova Scotia before emigrating to the US), and because the culture in a small East Coast town is completely different than a city, I knew I wanted to set a story in such a place. That culture not only defines what happens in the story, it also defines the characters.

However, when it came to the setting for the next book, *There was a Crooked Man*, this was borne because my pastor was contemplating buying a property in New Mexico and turning it into a retreat center for pastors.

Having my main character, Carly Turnquist, start out in her town of Bear Cove, Maine, then travel to New Mexico meant I wanted the next book to be set back in Bear Cove, which is why *Unbalanced* was set around not only that small-town lifestyle and mindset, but also the larger regional city which tends to govern and sometimes bully the smaller towns.

And then we come to Book 4, *Five and Twenty Blackbirds*, which releases April 30th. In this adventure, Carly and husband Mike visit the area where my dad and step-mother were married. While I prefer setting my books in fictional towns, Raven Valley is fashioned after the town of Cave Creek, Arizona. Both my father and step-mother are now with the Lord, so when I read this story, I feel their presence and influence on my life, for which I am grateful.

In Book 5, we're back in Bear Cove, Maine, with *Broke, Busted, and Disgusted*. Mike is missing, his client is dead, and Carly's up to her ears in debt. Not only that, but a dear friend has fallen under the spell of a con man. Bringing the story back to Carly's hometown lets me include some favorite characters while still introducing new people into her life.

Book 6, *Hidden Assets*, finds Carly in Wyoming as she helps a friend through a painful divorce. I chose this setting because I like this part of Wyoming and had recently been there. I have dear friends who live in the area, and we've done a bunch of research up there. Plus, I had the chance to create two more fictional towns, and ride the train vicariously with Carly, thanks to a friend's recent train experience that sparked this story.

And Book 7, *Petty Cash,* finds Carly and her family in Cape Cod, in the midst of a murder investigate, a counterfeiting operation, and missing grandchildren. Having visited the Cape a number of years ago, I thought this would make a nice setting for this book. I created a fictitious town but referenced several real towns on the Cape.

Takeaway: Think about the setting as another character in your story, and make plans to develop it completely.

Exercises:
1. Decide whether you want to use a real place or make one up.
2. Reveal the details of the setting through each character. How would a female in her 60s, for example, describe a barn as compared to how her ten-year-old grandson would describe it?
3. Find ways for the setting to direct the story so the characters have to react to that direction.

Defining Historical Fiction

One of the most popular genres in fiction writing continues to be historical, which spans, of course, all of history. Each period has its own sub-genres, along with its own set of reader expectations. Although there is general agreement on what constitutes a particular sub-genre, sometimes a publisher will be the deciding factor. For example, books set after World War 2 were rarely classified as historical until recent years. Now many publishers label books set up to and including the end of the Vietnam War as historical.

As with any other genre of fiction writing, knowing what genre and sub-genre your book fits into is important. First of all, acquisitions editors want to know because they need to be able to "sell" it to their publishing board. Unless the publisher is one of the big five or six, most will not publish multiple authors in the same genre in the same year. Secondly, book stores need to know where to file the book on their shelves. Also, online retailers will need to know what keywords to include in their descriptions for online buyers.

And all of this filters down to the reader: while a reader may read more than one genre, when they pick up a book, they want to know when and where that story is set. If they didn't get at least the time period from the genre description, they may not pick up the book. And some readers stick exclusively to historic fiction, some even to the point of reading only Biblical fiction, Tudor, Regency, Victorian, Colonial, Western, World War 1, World War 2, or the more modern historicals set between 1950 and 1970.

Another quirk in the equation is that as the years go by, the definition for historical will change. In ten years, historical might include the Central American drug wars and the Miami drug wars of the 1980s.

A recent question that has arisen is does the genre include only books written long after the event takes place, or do books written in that period now become historical because of the passage of time. For example, *The Great Gatsby* was written within just a few years of when the events happened, but now that is more than 90 years ago. We might consider that historical, but is it truly? Perhaps historical fiction can only be appreciated when written from a point of view where the author has the benefit of all that happened after the event.

The only thing we can count on about historical fiction is that while the history doesn't change, the definition of what constitutes the genre will.

Takeaway: Different publishers define historical fiction in different ways.

Exercises:
1. Go to the local bookstore and browse the shelves by category. See what publishers are publishing and make a note to check their website to see what they're looking for next.
2. Join a writer's group that is either specific to your genre or has authors who write what you write.
3. Write the story you want to write, and worry about the genre later.

Fact or Fiction — Choosing Your Setting

So you have a great idea for a book. You've done some character sketches. You know where the story is going. The only thing that's left, apart from the writing, is to decide where to set your book.

Your hometown? No, too many people know you there. That little town where you went on vacation last year? You loved the soda shop, the green grocer's on the corner, the barber with the cool twirling red, white, and blue sign. And what about the man at the post office? All the stories he told you about bank robbers and—wait a second. Was the main street through town called Main Street? Too boring. You want a street name that goes with the title of your book. Something more literary, more foreshadowing.

Scrap that town.

But wait a minute. Maybe not. Maybe that town is perfect. Except for the Main Street thing. And the fact that Pelican Lane—perfectly aligned with your book's character arc, by the way—runs the wrong direction.

What's a writer to do?

Simple. Do what you do best. Make up a town. Sure, draw from a town that you liked so well. But give it a new name. And while you're at it, maybe it needs to be in another state.

I choose to set all my books in fictional towns for a couple of reasons. I don't want to be constrained by what a real setting would be, and I like to make things up.

Blame it on the writer in me.

So go ahead. Put on your thinking cap. And make up a town. Or a city. Or an entire world.

Takeaway: It's your story, your world. Feel free to create your own.

Exercises:
1. Look at your book and the title and come up with something that goes with it. For example, in the fourth installment of my Carly Turnquist mysteries, *Five and Twenty Blackbirds*, Carly and Mike are at Mike's college reunion in Raven Valley, AZ. The college team mascot is a blackbird, so Raven Valley was pretty close.

2. Check to make sure there isn't a town by that name in that state by searching on the internet.
3. Look at towns near your desired setting to see how they are laid out. You can visit the area, and you can also go on Google Maps and look at the Earth View of addresses in the real town.

Interviewing Your Characters

"Getting to know you, getting to know all about you. . . "

When I sit down to create characters for a new project, this tune runs through my head. This is one truth writers ought to embrace: we need to know our characters better than anybody in our book does. Better than our readers will know them by the time they finish reading.

If we don't know our characters, we'll tend to write flat, one-dimensional people, like paper dolls who are simply wearing an outfit called "their story", and are as interchangeable as—well, a paper doll.

Another danger in not knowing our characters is we'll write three chapters getting to know them, wasting paper and the reader's time as we plow our way through their backstory, their history, until we finally get to the point where our story really starts, about halfway through Chapter 4.

There are many methods to get to know your characters. Some of these require you to sit down and fill out a questionnaire that would cause most of us to lose our minds or at the very least, our excitement about our stories. While the details and minutiae of these questionnaires might work for some, many of us will struggle to answer what our character's third grade teacher said that made him decide to become a private investigator twenty years later.

Bored with filling out forms, making up answers to questions I hadn't even thought of, and wanting to get on with the process of writing, I came up with a faster and more direct way to get to know my characters—I interview them.

I pretend I'm a famous talk show host and my character is a guest on my show. As a famous talk show host, I know everybody in the world will want to hear what I have to say and how I can make my character squirm on live TV. So I come up with questions that will cause said squirming because I know how the story goes and what secrets my character is trying to keep.

Go ahead. Be catty. Be devious. Dig up the dirt. What would someone who reads one of those supermarket tabloids want to know about your character? And why would your character not want to tell the truth, not want to break a confidence, not want you to know everything about them? Because characters are real people, and real people rarely tell the whole truth and nothing but the truth.

Even good people hide some things, hold back some things, try to make themselves look good perhaps at the expense of another.

Here is a list of questions I typically ask to get started:

1. How did you get the job you have?
2. What's your background that qualified you for that job?
3. Tell me about _____ (the inciting incident in the book).
4. Tell me about _____ (could be the love interest, the villain, the hero/heroine. Whoever is making this character's life difficult or messy in some way)
5. Tell me about _____ (whatever you know your character doesn't want to talk about. A past hurt, a secret, a rumor, an innuendo – anything that will make it look like this character isn't telling all)
6. Bring up a topic that's in the news now, and tie it into this character and the plot in some way. For example, if the character is a forest ranger, and poaching by forest rangers is in the news, ask what he thinks should be done to poachers and then what should be done to poachers who are also guardians of the woodland. Watch him squirm.
7. Ask what the character sees in his/her future.

By the time you ask and your character answers these questions, you should have a good idea of what motivates your character, what scares your character, what your character is trying to hide and why, the lie your character believes, what the internal and external conflicts are, and the growth arc of your character.

Takeaway: A character sketch is only as good as the questions asked.

Exercises:
1. Come up with a list of questions.
2. Interview your main character(s) and your villain(antagonist).
3. Be willing to dig deep. Ask lots of questions that will bring out your character's backstory, even though most of it won't go into the book.

Memories and Memoirs

My father had an interesting life story as well as an interesting family story. When he approached me to write these two stories down, I took him up on the offer. He understood that his story wasn't unique, yet the people were. His goal was to get the details down for the family as a keepsake.

Structuring a memory-based memoir poses some problems that are not unique to stories, and include:

1. Who is the story about? Figure out who your main characters are, and what you want the reader to know about them.
2. Who is telling the story? I decided that to get into the essence of the characters, there will be three sections in this book: his biological mother's story, his story, and his reunion with his half-brothers and –sisters.
3. Where to start? You can go chronological, which is how most stories are told. Or you can start at the end. Or perhaps start at a pivotal point in the middle and then go both forward and backward.
4. How much truth? The best you can do is research the setting and the people, then go forward from there. Fill in the gaps so long as it's possible the event might have happened.
5. What about if the truth hurts someone? Changing the facts or the names has legal ramifications, which you might want to check out with an attorney.

Takeaway: Every book has a basis in truth that lends to great storytelling techniques.

Exercises:
1. Read some memoirs to study structure, creative writing techniques, and what is told and what's left out.
2. Pick a story you want to tell. Brainstorm some title ideas.
3. Talk to family and get their input for what should go into the book and what should be left out.

People Just Like Me—and You

My tagline is "stories that brighten your day" because I like to read and write stories that don't just answer a burning question, or educate, or even pass the time. I like to read and write stories that brighten my day, give me hope, and strengthen me to keep on going when everything within me is screaming to simply give up.

Because underneath, I think most people are just like me. I have a husband, children, grands, siblings, various other friends and family who expect time and energy from me. I have a job, chores I'm responsible for, and not enough down time. Sometimes I question my faith, wonder if I really hear from God, worry that I don't spend enough time in prayer or Bible study, struggle with balancing my calendar.

And that's who I write about—people just like me. In my recent Christmas-themed release, *In Search of Christmas Past*, my heroine and hero both want something—but they don't want the same thing. Add into the mix the fact that my heroine is angry with God for not answering her prayers, but my hero has a real, alive, and growing relationship with God, and you can see where some conflict might crop up.

If we're honest, as believers, we've all been where my characters are—uncertain, pining for something more, wishing for things to be the way they used to be. We all go through change, and face it, we don't really like it.

But the good news is that with God in our camp, as our focus and the center of all the choices we make, we can get through this. I recently spoke with a new widow in our church, and I said how much she blessed me by being in church the first Sunday after her husband's funeral and in the choir the previous Sunday. She said, "How could I do anything else? God is my life. Brian (name changed) was my husband, but God is my life."

Her words encouraged me and strengthened me. It can be difficult to find joy in the midst of what seems like the darkest moment we'll ever face. And some moments are longer than that—they are seasons. My friend's life is forever changed with the passing of her husband, but she has learned a valuable lesson—God is bigger than the moments, bigger than the seasons.

And so I'll keep on writing about people just like me—and you. And I'll keep learning—and sharing—whatever God has for me to learn and apply.

Takeaway: God has a message for readers that only YOU can communicate.

Exercises:
1. List several traumatic life events that changed you.
2. List several uplifting life events that changed you.
3. How can you incorporate these events into a story?

Research Isn't Work

I always thought history was boring, probably because about the only thing I remember is memorizing dates for the reigns of monarchs (I'm from Canada, so we focused on British history). And I don't do well with memorizing.

But give me a tidbit of historical information, like the Pony Express, and I'm off to the races. And while not all research is historical, I thought you might be interested in a list of places where you can do research.

1. Your local library: most libraries have a local history section or a genealogy section, and in larger towns and cities, you will likely also find newspaper archives. Look for books written during the time period you're writing about.

2. Historical societies: often have diaries and journals of residents, albums of pictures, and lots of newspaper and magazine clippings. Most do a calendar each year as a fund raiser, so ask for back copies that are probably reduced in price now.

3. Historical markers: most states have dozens of historical markers along the highways. Don't be afraid to get off the highway for a few miles and follow a rutted trail into the middle of a huge meadow to discover a single marker about an obscure Civil War Battle that few have heard of.

4. Trail Interpretation Centers: not only do they talk about the trail but usually they include history of the local area as well.

5. Visitor Centers: often the people who work or volunteer at these centers are locals who know the local history or have an interest in a special piece of history.

6. State Park centers and gift shops: the people who work here usually know a lot about the area, or know the people in the area who know a lot.

7. Museums: there are museums for just about every interest. I have visited airplane and glider museums; Pony Express museums; Old Western Town museums; War museums; aircraft carrier museum; police and military museum; firearms museums; stagecoach museum; carriage museum; and automobile museums.

8. History Museums: particularly in larger cities, these museums bring in and rotate through a variety of exhibits during the year. Become a member and get on their mailing list to stay up to date. For example, Denver recently had the Sherlock Holmes exhibit and the Poison exhibit.

9. Entertainment attractions: for example, in Las Vegas, there are virtual reality-type shows where you can be a CSI and walk through a crime scene, look at evidence, and enter a report as to your findings.

10. Movies: I like to watch movies set in the time period I'm currently writing in. The closer the movie was made to the event the better, I've found.

For a recent release, *Echoes of the Heart,* I spent a lot of time in museums, in the library, online, and in the car driving from one Pony Express station to the next. While I haven't covered the entire trail, I hope to. Which will probably germinate more stories about the Pony Express.

Takeaway: No research is wasted.

Exercises:
1. Have you done a lot of research on a particular topic? Maybe you should become an 'expert' in this area and write about it often.
2. Is there a place you like to do research? Maybe it isn't the research but the place that could become the seed of a story. For example, a book about a museum curator who loses a priceless artifact who must prove she didn't steal it.
3. Is there a subject you struggled with in school? Maybe if you take a new look at it, you'll find you enjoy it now.

Setting the Tone for a Series

When I wrote the first book in the By the Numbers series, I had two things: a character and a title. Except the title wasn't *No Accounting for Murder*. My title was *Just the Fax, Ma'am*. But when I sent the book out to beta readers, one comment was it didn't say anything about the genre. That the title needed something to do with accounting, since that was an unusual character career, and the fact it was a cozy mystery.

I already knew a bunch of stuff about my main character, Carly Turnquist: she was exactly like me.

Well, not exactly, but pretty close. She is an accountant; I am an accountant. She is married to a computer programmer; check. This is her second marriage; check. She has two step-children who are the children of her heart; mine are both daughters, but check. She was married to an abusive alcoholic; check except my ex's problem was drugs. She lives in a small east coast town; I grew up on the east coast of Canada and know enough about small towns to write about them. And if I had any doubts, I could always refer to the Bible for Cozy Mystery Writers -- the Jessica Fletcher series.

However, when I got to the end of the first book, it seemed logical to take her into another, because I hadn't quite completed my character arc with her. She wasn't satisfied with where she was, and neither was I. I felt I needed to complete not just the story arc but also Carly's arc as well.

One thing I knew for sure about my book--because when I wrote the first one I wasn't thinking about a series--is that Carly doesn't take herself too seriously. And the only exercise she gets is jumping to conclusions. And she can't stay away from a mystery. Just like me.

And that's exactly the kind of series I wanted to write. To maintain that, I had to make some choices regarding titles, other plots points and characters, and the level of suspense in the books. I often describe the tone of the series as tongue-in-cheek. Carly is a little sassy (that's me, too), but much quicker on the comebacks than I could ever be, mostly because the writing enables me to think about a retort longer than would be practical in a conversation. My titles tell the reader that there is something going on, it's not just a missing hymnbook kind of mystery, but something a little darker, little more sinister below the surface, while still maintaining the gentleness of a cozy. To stay in line with genre expectations, murders happen off-stage, and there isn't much description of body parts and gore. But I try to make sure the suspense and tension are still there, mostly in the form of danger to the character, their family, their reputation, their credibility, their property.

One beta reader complained because there was no romance. "My characters are married" was my response, but really, isn't that where the best romance should be? Inside marriage? So I upped the romance between Carly and her husband, not by describing bedroom scenes, but by letting the imagination flow. Face it, we all know how it's done. I focus on the interaction more than the action.

The interesting thing is I've been continuing to learn new things about Carly as I write about her, things that weren't important before. For example, in *Five and Twenty Blackbirds*, I learned what college she graduated from; that she had a short crush on another student who went on to work for The Mob; and that she had a less-than-perfect side to her in college, something this Mob accountant is now holding over her in this book.

So as you set the tone for your series, here are a few things to keep in mind:

1. You don't need to know all the book plots in the series
2. Choose your main character with care--you're going to spend a lot of time with him or her
3. Choose an interesting occupation, something your readers will want to know more about. This opens the doors to describing what they do without boring them to tears
4. Decide on the tone so that all books are similar. You can vary the amount of tension and suspense in each book by changing up the levels of personal danger, but you don't want to have a beheading on stage in book 3, for example, while the first two books were about lost kittens and kidnapped puppies.
5. Listen to your beta readers. They read books like yours, and they usually know what they're talking about.
6. Be true to your genre and your story no matter what the market says is selling. I choose not to write erotica or use cussing because that's not who I am, and it's not what I want to read. Yet both seem to fill the bestseller lists. The interesting thing is that books without erotica and cussing are often better-written.

Takeaway: The decision to write a series should be made by the time the first book is finished.

Exercises:
1. In your current work-in-process, is there some plot line or character arc not completed? If so, you may have a series.
2. When planning a series, each book must lead to the next. Write the final scene of your book with that in mind.
3. Check out other series in your genre to see how the author refers to previous books and segues into the next book.

The Lies We Believe

(Excerpt from *Echoes of the Heart*, included in The Pony Express Romance Collection, a historical romance from Barbour Publishing, April 2017)

Catherine gathered her wilted skirts, straightened her hat, and stepped from the coach. The shotgun rider offered her a hand, which she gratefully accepted. The dry ground felt hard as cobblestones beneath her buttoned-up boots, and the hem of her dress attracted dust like a magnet. . .

Beneath her feet, the ground rumbled, and she hesitated. She'd heard of earthquakes in San Francisco, but surely not here. A stampede of cattle? Buffalo? Heart pounding, throat too dry to utter a sound, she glanced around, frantic to locate the source of the tremors. Should she run? Should she stand her ground?

Uncertain what to do, she remained frozen in place.

And still, to her right, the strange man with the brown felt hat remained rooted in place like a windblown scarecrow in a newly-planted field.

A shout, and she wheeled to her left.

A scream.

And not just any scream.

Her scream.

###

Benjamin sensed the incoming Pony Express rider before he saw him. The hooves pounded on the sunbaked trail, heralding the boy's arrival but his own feet weighed a hundred pounds each, rendering him unable to help the young woman who had alighted from the stage. Who was she? And why was she bringing her luggage with her?

The young woman stepped into the path of the rider, mere feet from those flashing hooves and half-ton of horseflesh, unmindful of the danger.

He stepped forward, dragging his cumbersome appendage behind him. In his mind, he saw himself running across the twenty or so feet separating them. But the reality of his movement jerked him back to the present

He would not reach her in time.

Instead, his stockman dropped her bag, whirled about, and covered the distance in four long strides. Wrapping an arm around her waist, Jake pulled her from the path of the oncoming horse and rider just in time.

The two stood together for what seemed like hours before Jake released his grip on her and resumed his task of taking her luggage into the way station.

Benjamin hurried over as fast as his straight leg would allow as she reached the first step leading into the station. "Ma'am, are you all right?"

Her hazel, tear-filled eyes lifted to meet his, holding his gaze.

She nodded.

He tipped his hat to her. "I'm glad you weren't injured. The way station yard can be a dangerous place. You mustn't allow your attention to wander."

Her mouth tightened into a hard line. "Perhaps you could ask your riders to be more considerate of those who live here."

Live here? What was she talking about? He cleared his throat. "Nobody lives here, ma'am, except me and Jake my stockman."

Not exactly true, of course. The Hollenbergs lived here. But she wasn't going to be here long enough to know about them.

She pulled her shoulders back as though defying him to correct her. "I am Margaret Thomas, Mr. Troudt's fiancée. And when Mr. Troudt finds the time to show his face, he'll confirm that fact for you."

Benjamin's mind raced. Surely this woman was mentally unbalanced. "I *am* Mr. Troudt. Benjamin Troudt. Station master. And either you are mistaken or misinformed. No woman lives here. I am not engaged to marry."

In the above excerpt, we see a prime example of miscommunication. Catherine, traveling under her best friend's name, believes she's answering an advertisement for a mail order bride, while Benjamin awaits the arrival of an older housekeeper. They both have secrets which keep them a prisoner to their past, because they both believe a lie spoken over them which won't allow them to enter into the close relationship God longs to have with them and threatens to keep them from experiencing their happily-ever-after.

We all have secrets that we'd be embarrassed if someone else knew, and we all believe a lie that hinders our relationship with God and with others. Just as with Catherine and Benjamin, we have to recognize the lie for what it is, understand that God already knows everything, and be willing to trust Him as we go forward in our lives.

Takeaway: We must open our hearts to hear the truth that will always confound the lie.

Exercises:
1. What lies do you believe about yourself that don't line up with scripture?
2. What scripture verses can you use to counter those lies?
3. Pray the Lord reveal all the lies so you can arm yourself against them.

The Therapy Couch

Developing a main character for your novel can be like trying to identify the perfect, already-house-trained never-will-chew-on-your-shoes won't-keep-you-up-all-night-barking-or-howling Labrador puppy from a litter of a hundred identical little balls of fur.

You can't really tell what the finished product is going to be like until you live with it for a while.

As writers, how do we live with our characters? We write about them. We talk to them. We let them talk to us. We let them surprise us when they do something we weren't expecting. We keep on writing when they reveal some aspect of their past we knew nothing about, even though we're secretly peeved. Having a character hold out on you can be like having your best friend keep a secret.

Another really cool way I've discovered to examine your character and get down to the nitty-gritty of who they are and what drives them is through an analysis. Jeannie Campbell at http://charactertherapist.com offers a great service where you answer questions about your character's background and life, and she offers insight into what actually constitutes your character's Goal, Motivation, and Conflict. She is a licensed family and marriage counselor, and for a small fee, she will provide you at least 3 pages of analysis for your character.

Investing in this analysis can save your sanity – really. Your characters will be more realistic, your plot will flow smoother, and you will come away with a better structured novel. In addition, she has a blog, a newsletter, free articles on writing, and she offers several eBooks on grief, personality types and disorders, and on creating rich back stories.

When I submitted my questionnaire to her about my character, Betsy Rollins, a feisty Colorado rancherwoman who has been "guilted" into taking over the family ranch when all she really wants to do is enjoy her retirement, Jeannie came back with an in-depth analysis of my character, which, I'll admit, was a little autobiographical—aren't most of our characters? She also included several suggestions on scenes that would strengthen the reader's understanding of why my character does what she does, and a scene where my character will be confronted by a conflict between her behavior and her intentions – always a sure way to build conflict within your character.

Check out her website, again, it's http://charactertherapist.com and tell her I recommended you visit. She'll remember me. I'm the one who retrieved my stolen bicycle and got a little payback at the same time.

Takeaway: Having your main character visit a psychologist can be liberating!

Exercises:
1. There are lots of website that offer character analysis. Check out the internet and pick one.
2. If you don't feel comfortable sharing with a stranger, write a character sketch with backstory, and pass it through your critique group, asking for their input.
3. Apply whatever feedback you get.

What's in a Name?

You've heard the old saying, "a rose by any other name is still a rose". And I guess when we're talking flowers, that would true.

But what about when we're talking titles? Would you rather read *Tote the Weary Load* or *Gone with the Wind*? The first was a working title for Margaret Mitchell.

The truth is, whether we like it or not, a catchy title will make our work stand out from the rest of the pack. Here are some questions to ask in coming up with a good handle for your book:

1. What is the book about? The plot, the conclusion, or the setting can make for a good title. For example, *War of the Worlds*, *The Last of the Mohicans*.

2. Choose a main character, and change how the reader sees him. For example, would you read *Holden Caulfield* or *Catcher in the Rye*?

3. Change the meaning of a word. For example, a book where the heroine finds herself in the middle of a battlefield could be called *Grace in the Midst of War*, if the character's name is Grace. And if it isn't, you might like the title and so change the character's name.

4. Choose groupings of three: *The Good, The Bad, and The Ugly*, for example. A book in my forensic accountant mystery series is titled *Broke, Busted, and Disgusted*.

5. Choose the theme of the book. I wrote a novel about a crooked cop who desperately wants to go straight, and all the while, everybody thinks he's a good guy: *Counterfeit Honor*.

6. Consider your genre and pump up the title accordingly. The first book in my forensic accountant mystery series was originally titled *Just the Fax, Ma'am* because some threatening faxes are at the core of the story. However, a beta reader said she wouldn't pick up the book because there was no connection to a mystery. Now the book is titled *No Accounting for Murder*.

No matter what title ideas you come up with, pass them by some people you trust, including your beta readers, critique group, and writing groups you may belong to. Sometimes taking a word from one, a word or two from another, and recombining them gives you a whole new idea. Whatever the title is, you want to draw readers in with the title, but the writing will be what keeps them reading.

Takeaway: A good title makes all the difference.

Exercises:
1. Make a list of phrases to describe your book. Would one of them make a good title?
2. Make a list of character names and look for ways to incorporate that into the title.
3. Consider the characters and the plot; is there a way to make a 'play' on words to create a compelling title?

Write What You Know

Writers hear this all the time at conferences: write what you know.

As a new writer, I took this advice seriously.

So when I sat down to write my first book, I asked myself: what do you know?

I knew numbers.

I was trained as a bookkeeper, had worked for many years in accounting departments, and I love numbers.

I like the fact that they are constant and consistent, that 1 and 1 always equals 2, despite that old accountant's joke: what is 1 and 1? Answer: what do you want it to be?

But accountants are boring, right? If you tell someone you're a teacher, they ask, "oh, what grade?" If you tell them you're a doctor, they want to know if you can help them with the pain in their back. And if you tell them you're a writer, they want to know what you've published.

But an accountant? Eyes glaze over, and they suddenly find someone else they just have to talk to.

But accounting and numbers I knew. And I could see that might be a skill that could come in handy for solving crimes. So I did some research into what kind of bean counters helped solve crimes.

And I learned that forensic accountants do exactly that.

They are hired by the IRS, by divorce and estate attorneys. They work as investigators. Think of the movie, *The Untouchables*. Who was the real hero? Not Kevin Costner and Sean Connery, although they are two of my favorite actors. No, the mousy little accountant is the one who figured out how to take down one of the greatest mobsters of all time, Al Capone.

By looking at numbers.

They got Big Al on tax evasion.

The tagline for my series is: *Most people think accountants are boring; Carly Turnquist is about to prove them wrong.*

Because I'm an accountant, and as my husband tells me, I am anything but boring.

Takeaway: You don't have to be an expert to write with credibility.

Exercises:
1. Make a list of what you know.
2. Make a list of what you like to read.
3. Create a character that does something from the first question in a genre related to an item from the second.

Write What You Want to Know

We've all heard "write what you know", and that's all well and good as far as it goes. But what happens if what you know could fill a thimble? Or if what you know is already well-written by others? Do you simply stop writing?

No!

That's the time when you step out and write what you want to know.

That's the time you do some research into a topic that's always interested you. That's the time you branch out from what you know and specialize. For example, let's say you are a bank teller, so you know about banking policies and procedures. Might make an interesting main character in a book or a series. *Firewall*, with Harrison Ford, was one such movie.

But let's take your knowledge a little deeper. You've had training in spotting counterfeit currency and negotiable documents, so maybe that's who your character is. You've had training in investments, so maybe your character is an investment banker. "Wait," you say, "I don't know anything about that."

So now's the excuse—and the time—to learn.

And here's the great thing about research—you can also research settings. Say you have a great idea for a counterfeiter-turned-honest but you want the story set in San Jose, California because you need to be close to a naval base because your character has to try to break into a naval base with counterfeit documents. But you've never been to San Jose, CA.

That's the time you take a trip there. Take lots of pictures, map out the city, pick where your hero lives, where he works, where he goes to the gym—decide where would make great settings for scenes, and go there. Now when you write about San Jose, your writing will have a layer of credibility you couldn't have gotten any other way.

Writing what you know and writing where you know is always a good place to start, but when you need something new, think about writing what you want to know and where you want to go.

Takeaway: Since you won't know more than you do know, feel free to branch out in your writing.

Exercises:
1. Make a list of occupations you don't know much about.
2. Make a list of settings you've never been to.
3. Select one from each list and do some research.

Writing A Novella

The rule of thumb for plots in standard-length novels is 30,000 to 40,000 words should contribute to the main plot line with two main characters. Additional secondary but still important characters and each additional plot line adds another 10,000 words. So to get to a standard-length novel of 70,000 words, you would have the main plot and three to four subplots and/or secondary but still important characters.

And then there is the novella. A short novel. Should be easy to write, correct? After all, it's just an abbreviated version of a standard-length book.

Not so easy as you might think.

Most novellas contain one main plot, two main characters, and at least one subplot, which could total 50,000 based on the formula in the first paragraph. So how do you reduce the stories down to 30,000 or even 20,000 words?

I've read a few novellas, and many of them follow this pattern: regurgitate the entire backstory in the first five pages, then spend the rest of the book telling me what the characters want.

The better ones follow a different formula, which I also incorporate into my novellas. This alternate pattern keeps the action moving, keeps the reader reading, and keeps the pages turning:

1. Sprinkle the backstory in little by little. For example, in a recent novella, *Echoes of the Heart*, for The Pony Express Romance Collection from Barbour Publishing, I allude to the fact that my heroine, Catherine, had to leave Boston, without telling the reader why until later in the story.

2. Don't put any backstory details in until after chapter 2.

3. Have the hero and heroine meet in the first chapter. Limit the subplot to one. In *Echoes,* my subplot centers on a Pinkerton agent who is looking for a mysterious woman who lures men to her room then robs them.

4. Connect the subplot to the main plot. In *Echoes,* at one point, the hero thinks the heroine is this woman. And then the heroine thinks the Pinkerton agent is after her because of some stolen property she is holding.

5. Know your word count and chapter count before you start: then you can calculate the average words per chapter. Knowing this means you won't have too much happening in your chapters, and you won't be tempted to introduce a new plotline halfway through the book, which is very common in standard-length novels.

6. Be willing to cut: your first draft might go beyond your allowed word count. Don't worry. You can always cut some description and dialogue in your edit. Dialogue should be short and pithy. Incomplete sentences. Veiled innuendoes.

7. Keep your internal dialogue to a minimum: Don't have the point of view character think something and then say it out loud or worse yet, don't reiterate it in narrative.

8. Keep your points of view limited to your two main characters: the more points of view you include, the more words you use. Use other techniques to keep your main characters in the dark, rather than having action happen off-stage. For example, in *Echoes*, I have my hero overhear the tail end of my heroine's prayer such that he thinks she wants to leave because of him.

As you can see, there are many ways to limit your words while increasing the impact of your story. Foreshadowing, miscommunication, limited backstory, and limited plot lines all contribute to a great read.

Takeaway: You can tell a powerful story in as little as six words, perhaps fewer.

Exercises:
1. Practice writing short. Write a complete story in 100 words or less.
2. Search the internet for flash fiction and see the techniques used to write compelling stories with few words.
3. Write a synopsis with one major plot and one subplot.

Writing a Series

When first sitting down and staring at the blank screen or page before you, it might be difficult to even think you have more than one book in you. However, if you want to write a series, there are some things to do to set that up in the first book:

1. If your main character has more than one story to tell, you have a series.
2. Develop a character arc for each book, taking a series of small steps toward accomplishing the goal of this story and one or two steps toward the overall arc of the series.
3. Stick to one main plot and usually no more than three subplots. Save the rest for the next books.
4. The last sentence of the book should point toward the next story, even if you haven't written word one yet.
5. Include the first chapter of the next book as a sneak peak at the end of each book to remind readers this is a series and that yes, there will be another book this side of the new millennium.

Takeaway: You don't need a huge story idea to write a series.

Writing the Story

Cutting Extra Words

So you've gotten to the end of your novel, and you check the number in the lower left-hand corner of your screen (if you're working in MS Word), and yikes! What should have been a 90,000-word novel is now a 112,000-word tome. For those of you who struggle with every single word, you might think I'm kidding about having *that* too-many words. I'm not.

But as writers we love every single one of those words, so how can we possibly think of taking any out, of effectively leaving them on the cutting room floor, to coin a film-production phrase.

We can't. But we must.

Not only do fewer words mean fewer pages which translates into more profit, but fewer words can also mean—gulp!—a better telling of a much better story.

How does that happen? In several ways.

First, writers often tell readers the same information many times throughout the story. Nothing loses me quicker than to read, for the fifth time, "and if she couldn't have him, no other woman would". I got it the first time. Readers are smart. They get it.

Second, some writers love to spell out every nuance of every detail of every object in the setting at hand. And they tell readers in as many ways as their thesaurus or synonym finder can tell them. Readers don't want to read the amplified version of your story. They don't need to hear that your tiny, petite, svelte, athletic, feminine, frilly, girly-girl heroine has eyes the color of the azure blue of the Mediterranean Sea where it touches the toe of Greece. See how many adjectives I used here?

Third, some things are best not said at all, as your mother used to tell you. Backstory is one example. Do not introduce backstory for at least the first fifty (or so) pages, unless you are writing a novella, and then hold back for at least ten pages. Also, you don't need to describe your characters like you're reading off their driver's license. Instead, show us your character through what they're wearing, through their wardrobe choice or posture, through the car they drive or the books they read.

This is my process for cutting extra words:

- If there are two adjectives, choose the strongest. For example: dark, brown hair => chocolate hair

- Every additional character adds about 10,000 words, so consider combining characters. For example, if you need a fire fighter and a best friend for the heroine, consider a female fire fighter.
- Every additional subplot adds about 20,000 words, so consider cutting a subplot. Maybe there is one that could stand alone, so cut that one. Maybe there is one that introduces additional characters, so cutting that one might also eliminate more words because of the point above.
- Look for redundant phrases, such as: stand up; sit down, shrugged his shoulders; nodded her head; heart pounded in his chest. Since we usually only stand or sit, shrug only our shoulders or nod our head, and our heart is never anywhere but our chest, we can eliminate those extra words.
- Look for intrusive phrases such as: he watched; she heard; he saw; she smelled. In deep point of view, we are already in the POV character's head. Just say what the character watched, saw, heard, smelled, etc.
- Change passive voice to active: in passive voice, the verb is weak and inactive. Instead, change it to a strong, active verb. Many times a passive verb can be identified by ending in 'ing'. For example: His shoes were besmirched with gore from the battle => Gore from the battle besmirched his shoes. (You cut 2 words and made the image more clear).

Takeaway: Readers may not recognize bad writing, but they will know they didn't get into the story like they usually do.

Exercises:
1. Check for backstory introduced too soon and move it later in the story.
2. Check for passive voice in sentence structure and change it to make it more active.
3. Do a search on '-ing' verbs and replace them with more active verbs.

The Action/Danger Hook

Everybody tells you that you need to grab a reader right from the start of the story so they get through the first few pages until they fall in love with your characters and want to finish the book.

One of the surest ways to keep a reader's attention is to use what's called an action/danger hook, which contains, as its name implies, both action and danger suitable to the genre and context.

The action doesn't all have to be physical, like car chases or trying to escape from a burning house. The action can be inner turmoil or decision-making. It can be anticipated, such as in foreshadowing. Or it can be slow and deliberate, such as sneaking up on a suspect.

The danger doesn't have to be physical, either. Emotional, spiritual, financial, and relational dangers are all perfectly acceptable.

The hook can tell the reader what danger is lurking, or it can foreshadow, but the best hooks I've seen cause the reader to ask a question, because then they want to keep reading to have that question answered.

The secret to using the action/danger hook is to mix them up so that your character isn't always left hanging off the edge of a cliff.

For example, the opening line in a book about a woman who is forced to marry after her husband dies might be:

Susie McAllister had sworn to herself that the next time she married, it would be for love. However, that was not to be.

Right away, the reader asks questions: what happened that she has to get married again? And why not for love? And why did she make that decision—is it because she didn't love her previous husband?

An action/danger hook I used at the end of my first book, *No Accounting for Murder*, was intended to lead the reader into the next in the series:

It would be nice to have a quiet vacation on a ranch. After all, what could go wrong?

Horseback riding, long walks, good food. She could catch up on some research and read that novel she'd bought a year ago.

Yes indeed, what could go wrong?

Use action/danger hooks in the first sentence of a book, the first sentence of a scene, the last sentence of a scene, and the first sentence of a chapter. If you're writing a series, you might also want to have the last couple of sentences propel the reader into the next book. We want to keep the reader reading, to not give them an excuse to stop. Vary the hooks so that they address the different arcs the characters are facing, and tailor them to the tone of the scene or chapter. For example, a more introspective scene would have a more introspective hook. Applying this technique to your story will keep the story—and the reader—moving.

Takeaway: Action/danger hooks keep readers reading.

Exercises:
1. Check every scene and chapter for an action/danger hook ending.
2. Check every scene and chapter for an action/danger hook opening.
3. If you're writing a series, one of your biggest action/danger hooks should be the end of your book. Check this.

The Opening Line

Readers are easily bored.

Hopefully that opening line caught your attention and did at least three things. The following can be applied to any written material, whether fiction or non-fiction, short story, epic novel, or flash fiction.

The opening line:
1. Introduces the topic: the opening sentence establishes a contract with the reader, lets them know what's coming, sets the tone, and weeds out those who aren't really interested in what you have to say. Because this one thing is true--not everybody will be part of your target audience, and the quickest way to lose a reader forever is to promise something you don't deliver.
2. Causes questions to arise: if you tell the reader everything they need to know in the opening line, they don't need to read the next 200 words or 200 pages. Instead, your opening line should cause questions to arise in the reader's mind. In this case: why are readers easily bored? How can I keep them from getting bored?
3. Makes the reader want to read more: When readers invest time and energy in your writing, they are less likely to give up, which offers you the opportunity to demonstrate what an excellent writer you are and what a compelling story you can weave. This, in turn, will transform your readers into fans and influencers for your products.

In Summary: you want your opening line to give a hint of what the story is about; cause the reader to ask at least one question that cannot be answered unless they continue reading. If you've accomplished that, you have written a great opening line. You do this by starting with action, identify the main character or situation the character finds herself in, and foreshadow what's to come.

Takeaway: The opening line will hook the reader, but the writing must keep them on the line.

Exercises:
1. Check your opening line—does it introduce the main character, the problem, and the conflict?
2. Does it make the reader ask questions?
3. Would you want to keep reading? If not, change it.

Wrapping a Not-So-Unique Story in a Unique Setting

Have you ever started to read a book where you got to the third chapter (or sooner) and tossed it aside because you weren't engaged?

To engage readers, writers often focus on developing multi-dimensional characters and character journeys and backstory, but we neglect that all-important setting.

When handled properly, setting becomes as much of a character as the people themselves. I recently completed my father's memoirs, a story of growing up in Newfoundland in the 1930's and 1940's. When most people hear "Newfoundland", they think of *Shipping News,* or, if they are of a 'certain' age, Farley Mowatt's *A Whale for the Killing.*

My father's story, which releases in the general market version in October as *The Physics of Love*, is nothing like either of those books.

His situation—learning that his 'sister' was actually his mother; that his father was actually his grandfather; that his biological father wanted nothing to do with him; and that the woman he called Mom wasn't even related to him by blood—are not unique in and of themselves.

What makes this story unique is the setting—a small outport town with few amenities and fewer luxuries, on an island with commercial ties to both Canada and the United States but with no official or governmental standing of its own. At the time of the start of this story, Newfoundland was a dominion in the British Empire, and wouldn't become part of Canada until 1949 after a hotly-contested and probably fixed election.

A unique setting accomplishes three things:

- It becomes a character on its own merits, as discussed above. Change the setting, change the story. *The Old Man and the Boat* is a completely different story than *Jaws*, although both involve boats and big fish.
- It adds depth to the people in the story as we learn why the characters made the choices they made—they had no other choice because of the setting, which can exert physical, emotional, or cultural forces.

- It exposes readers to a new set of life experiences that they wouldn't have experienced had the story been set elsewhere.

So in the next book you read, ask yourself if the setting is critical to the story, or if it could be set somewhere else. In *The Physics of Love*, for example, I could have set it in almost any small town in Newfoundland, but had I moved it to New York City, that would have changed the story completely.

If the setting is important, look for ways the author strives to enforce that idea. It doesn't simply happen by mentioning the name of the town or describing the setting in detail—importance is defined by how much it impacts the characters and their decisions.

Takeaway: Setting is an important character in any book.

Exercises:
1. Read a favorite book and look especially for setting descriptions.
2. Make a list of ways the setting in your story can cause conflict with the characters.
3. Do some research on your setting. This is called 'setting backstory'. Introduce it slowly through the story, in the same way you would character backstory.

Writing Your Family Story

A couple of years ago, I had the unhappy fortune to be with my father as he answered questions for the intake counselor at a hospice facility. He patiently answered her questions about his family, his children, what he'd done for a living, until he grew tired. And then he simply said, "If you want to know any more, read the book."

"Read the book?" She looked at each sibling. "What book?"

"There on the bookcase."

I handed her the book. "It's the first part of his life, up until he married my mom, and then the last part, where he found his half-siblings from his father's side of the family."

She thumbed through the book then she looked up at us again. "You won't believe how many family members come through here every year who say they wished they'd listened more closely to their parent's stories. Or how many parents who say they wished they'd taken time to write down the stories. This is the first time I've met anybody who actually did it. You have a treasure here."

Even if you don't think of yourself as a writer, you might want to record family stories for future generations. Here is the process we used to write the book for family only and then prepare it for the general market.

1. Decide what your goal is: first and foremost, this was a history book for the family. Secondly, he knew his story wasn't unique, but the setting and the characters were, and we felt that would set the book apart in the general market.

2. Decide the structure: he wanted to tell three separate stories including how he came to be born and placed in the family he was raised in, his life growing up in a unique setting, and finding his half-siblings on his birth father's side of the family. So we went with the three-books-in-one approach, from two different points of view, his birth mother's and his.

3. Decide what to include: a person's life has innumerable stories, so we kept to the ones that best described my father—pragmatic, logical, forward-thinking.

4. Decide whom to protect: in the family-only version, we toned down some stories where we felt we knew the truth but couldn't

prove it, while in the market version, we changed the names of the characters, kept the name of the town, and wrote it the way we believed it happened.

    5. Decide what to exclude: my father came to Christ three weeks before he passed away, so that was a huge part of the family-only book, even though it was a short part of his life on this earth. The title, *My Cup Has Overflowed*, came from a song I love called "I'm drinking from my saucer, Lord, because my cup has overflowed". We decided not to include much of that story in the market version.

So, if you're thinking about writing your family story, don't wait. If you're tired of hearing Uncle John's stories or Grandma Mary's tales, don't tune them out. Write the stories. They won't always be here.

Takeaway: Writing a family story is a great way to get to know more about your family.

Exercises:
1. Pay attention at your next family gathering. Jot down notes of the stories you hear.
2. Write out the stories you remember others telling you in the past.
3. Write out the stories from your own childhood you think your children and family would like to hear.

Story Structure

Create Questions in the Reader's Mind

Various marketing studies have shown that authors have about ten seconds to catch a reader's attention. From the time the reader picks up the book from the shelf in the book store, checks the back cover copy, flips to the first page, and reads that, ten seconds have elapsed.

Not a lot of time. Ten heartbeats. Four eye-blinks. Two swallows.

It passes quickly.

As authors, we know the first line has to grab the reader so they read the whole paragraph, and that has to keep their attention until they get to the end of the first page, which will hopefully propel them beyond the ten seconds and into the decision to purchase your book. And whether they are buying a print version or an electronic copy, the decision-making is the same.

So you work and polish and fine tune the manuscript.

But what about the back cover copy? Isn't that just a couple of hundred words you throw together at the end?

No, it's not. These couple of hundred words can make the difference between whether the buyer sets your book back or checks the inside to see the "important" stuff you wrote and edited and fine-tuned.

Here are some things to keep in mind about back cover copy:

1. Start thinking about it when the nugget of an idea for your book pops into your head. Keep thinking about it while you do whatever plotting, outlining, or synopsis-writing you do. Even if you don't do any of those things, picture the blurb on the back of your book. What font? How many words?

2. You want to highlight your main character(s), by telling the reader where the character(s) is at the beginning of the story, what the conflict is, who the antagonist is, and some idea of your main character(s) motivations. For example, if there is any romance in your story, tell the reader how the heroine can't abide people who lie but who stole from the employer who molested her to feed her little sister. And how your hero, who is a braggart who is also in law enforcement, can't abide thieves. And how when they're thrown together to find the little sister who is kidnapped by a pimp who wants to sell her as a sex

slave, your hero tries to keep her thievery a secret and he tries to keep his propensity to exaggerate a secret.

3. Now that you've set up the reader to care about these characters, to empathize with them--who hasn't lied or stolen at least once?--you want to give them a teaser about what happens next. For example, "Can Lisa find her sister before her sister is abused the way she was? And can Tom put aside his belief that thieves never tell the truth and trust Lisa? Or will they both lose the only things that are important to them?"

4. You don't want to give away the ending but you do want to tell enough so the reader knows there are big enough stakes to care about.

Takeaway: Readers keep reading because we create 'what is going to happen now?' questions for them.

Exercises:
1. Write a one-sentence summary of your current work-in-process.
2. Write a one-paragraph summary (three sentences) telling why the hero and heroine should connect, why they shouldn't connect, and end with a question about whether they will connect.
3. Write a one-page synopsis of your story outlining the major and secondary plot points, and how this connects the hero, the heroine, the protagonist, and the antagonist.

Entice Your Readers

I guest blog for a number of authors throughout the year, and one thing we've noticed is that readers are less likely to (a) read our blogs, (b) follow our blogs, and (c) leave a comment on our blogs.

That said, authors are still being told that blogging and social media is the best way to connect with readers.

However, the statistics don't speak to results.

If that is the case, then how do you entice your readers to read, follow, and comment?

You need to make it worth their while.

What do readers want to read about? Your next book, of course. For example, when I write a blog post, I try to mention that my most recent release. I tell them how my book will meet a felt-need—in other words, WHY they should read my book. As an example, *The Physics of Love* is the story of an unredeemable woman, a boy-child looking for a forever family and true love, and a man who found both. This is a 'felt-need' because in some way, we are all unredeemable, so we can empathize with this woman; we are all looking for relationships and love; and we want to read stories where the characters get what they think they want.

Readers want to learn more about your characters. These aren't just words on a page—these people are real to them. You can respond to this need by posting interviews with characters, let your characters answer some tough questions, or put your hero and antagonist in a room and let them duke it out.

You can also post short stories featuring your main characters. Perhaps a prequel story or a story between books. Offer these as a freebie to readers who subscribe to your blog or newsletter.

What don't readers want to read about? They don't want to hear another sales pitch—they get those all the time. They don't want to hear that your next book will be out in three years—they want that story yesterday! And while the reality is you can't put them out that fast, maybe you could do another series, another stand alone, to keep their appetite whetted for the next book.

You can offer them a free print book for leaving a comment or subscribing to your newsletter. Yes, you will spend a couple of dollars mailing said book and a few dollars for the print copy, but really—free eBooks abound on the internet. You must offer something more.

Another enticement is a personal visit with you, the author. Sure, you can't go traipsing around the country, but you can host a free webinar where readers can ask you questions about your writing process, where you come up with ideas, what's coming next. Treat it like a contest—after all, you're an author!

Run a contest that if a reader leaves a comment and an email address, you'll name a character after them in your next book. Or you'll set the book in their hometown. Or you'll include one of their kids in the story. Or all three.

Takeaway: Readers want to know WHY they should read your book. In other words, what's in it for them?

Exercises:
1. If you don't have an email list, start one. There are lots of great free services out there, including MailChimp. Come up with a short story or a first chapter to offer as an incentive.
2. Look for email list builders to participate in. Most cost $25 or less, but you could secure up to 1,000 new subscribers.
3. If you have a newsletter, think about swapping feature spots with other authors in your genre to introduce your readers to other authors, and to get an introduction to another author's readers.

Dialogue techniques

Dialogue breaks up the narrative, the exposition, the description. Dialogue is a great place to show conflict, set up foreshadowing, and fill in backstory.

Let's take a look at each of these purposes for dialogue.

1. Show conflict: we don't need fight scenes to show that two characters are at odds with each other. We can also do that through dialogue, both verbal and internal. Here's an example:

> Sally paused in the doorway. "Oh, Bob, I didn't expect to see you here. How are you doing?"
>
> Bob glanced up from his newspaper then returned to his crossword puzzle. "And why shouldn't I be here?"
>
> "I thought you were out of town this week."
>
> He peered at her over the top of his glasses. "Did you have something special planned while I was away?"

In this example, neither one answers the other's question directly. Both seem suspicious of the other. Bob's rude treatment by continuing his puzzle and then looking at her over his glasses implies something is going on, but their words could stand alone and you'd know there was some tension between these two characters.

Let's use internal dialogue to show conflict:

> Sally paused in the doorway. "Oh, Bob, I didn't expect to see you here. How are you doing?"
>
> She already knew the answer wouldn't be good. *Why do I even bother?*
>
> Bob glanced up from his newspaper then returned to his crossword puzzle. "And why shouldn't I be here?"
>
> "I thought you were out of town this week." That's what he'd said yesterday. Not that she could ever trust him to be honest with her.
>
> He peered at her over the top of his glasses. "Did you have something special planned while I was away?"

In this example, we see the exact same dialogue, but now we hear a little from Sally. She sounds weary of the conflict, whatever it is, and she doesn't trust Bob.

2. Set up foreshadowing: foreshadowing is the technique of alerting the characters and the reader that something is going to happen, or might happen.

> Marcus slumped in his chair. "I knew this day would come. And I knew I wouldn't be ready for it."
> "Don't be such a prognosticator." His wife rubbed his shoulders. "Sometimes I think you're the Grinch in disguise."
> He glanced at the empty mantel. "The kids are going to hate me."
> "And why should they do that?"
> He buried his face in his hands. "I feel like I've stolen their Christmas."

We see here that although his wife doesn't realize it, he feels like he is the Grinch who stole Christmas. Using this dialogue builds the tension in the scene until we get to the reveal.

3. Fill in backstory through dialogue, but never use "as you know" or over-explain the situation. The reader will get it.

> Maggie sat. "What aren't you telling me?"
> How was he going to explain without telling her his entire life story? Again. "I went to see at eleven."
> She nodded. "I know."
> He leaned forward, elbows resting on his knees. "What you don't know is that I died that same year."
> She gasped.
> "And I was reborn."
> "How?"
> "I recreated myself." He sat back. "Our lives are based on a lie. And someone besides me knows the truth. Which means we're in danger."

In this example, he starts with one thing she already knows, then progresses rapidly into six facts she didn't know: he died, he was reborn, he took on a false identity, he isn't who she thinks he is (their lives are a fabrication), somebody else has found out, and they are in danger.

Hopefully you've seen some new ways to use dialogue in your writing. It doesn't matter what genre you write, these techniques will enliven your dialogue and keep your readers turning pages.

Takeaway: Foreshadowing creates questions in the reader's mind, which keeps them turning pages.

Exercises:
1. Choose a scene in your manuscript where there's lots of dialogue, and introduce some inner dialogue to show tension.
2. Choose another scene in your manuscript, and add more dialogue.
3. Choose a scene where you've told the backstory in narrative form, and instead make it dialogue.

Romantic Tension

Sounds like an oxymoron, doesn't it? After all, who wants romance and tension at the same time? You do. I do. And readers do, too.

Romance draws your male and female protagonists together with promises of a happy ending inherent. Tension is what keeps them apart throughout the story, raises questions about whether they should be together, causes them to assess their goals and priorities, offers an opportunity for the antagonist to have a say in the matter, and keeps the story moving forward.

Face it, if boy meets girl, boy gets girl in the first chapter, the romance is pretty much tied in a knot for the rest of the story.

So how do we create the tension in a romance without having the characters constantly fighting, breaking up, and making up? One or two rounds of that in a story is more than enough.

Each character needs to have a backstory. Not about where he went to college or what kind of car she drives. This romantic backstory should include past relationships, the lie the character believes about themselves, their dreams or goals regarding their romantic future, and the obstacles that keeps them from achieving their romantic goal.

For example, Bob had a girlfriend in college who dumped him for a rich frat guy. The lie he believes is that no girl could possibly love him for himself; he needs to make lots of money and be successful. The problem is that the more he works and the more stuff he acquires, the less time he has for a girlfriend.

Sue longs to have the marriage her parents had. They fell in love in sixth grade and were together ever since. But, the guy she fell in love with in high school ended up getting her pregnant and then leaving her before the baby was born. The lie she believes is that there are no happily-ever-afters, and no man is going to want her. She's damaged goods. So she holds all men at arm's length.

In your story, you could have Bob meet Sue at work. He's attracted to her but manages to work through every date he makes with her, which confirms her belief that no man should be depended on. Sue doesn't tell Bob about her daughter, so she has to work hard to keep that secret, and when Bob finds out, he believes she's just like every other woman—out to take what she can get. After all, she probably tried to trick some poor guy into marrying her by getting pregnant.

Bob's beliefs and Sue's are at odds with each other. If they both stick to their guns, they won't get together.

Work them through their problems, get them to change their belief system, and get them together by the end of the book, or at least to a point where the reader understands there's a very good chance they will get together.

Takeaway: Tension and conflict are not the same thing.

Exercises:
1. What is the lie your hero believes? Construct a lie for your heroine that goes against the lie the hero believes.
2. What is the lie your antagonist or villain believes? Construct another like for your hero and heroine that would seek to prove the antagonist/villain wrong in their belief.
3. Pick a scene where your hero and heroine are arguing. Interject some internal dialogue that introduces some of the backstory of each character so the reader knows what they are *really* arguing about.

The Writing Life

Creating a Pseudonym

Several people have asked me "Why a pseudonym?", so I thought perhaps more readers and authors might want to know the answer, as well. Within the Christian community, I've had folks who said, "Isn't that like lying?"

The answer to the first question is perhaps easier than to the second. So I'll start with the second.

In the Bible, we see many instances of folks being given new names. Abram became Abraham and Sarai became Sarah because God changed who they were. Jacob became Israel, which loosely translated means "one who struggles with God" because of his night-long battle with the angel of the Lord. Joseph of the Old Testament was given a new name by the Pharaoh because of his new position, and in Isaiah 62:4 we read: Never again will you be called "The Forsaken City" or "The Desolate Land." Your **new name** will be "The City of God's Delight" and "The Bride of God," for the Lord delights in you and will claim you as his bride.

In Biblical times, names had a meaning, so it only makes sense that if God changes who we are in Him, it's not lying.

How does that apply to my pen name? Well, that brings us to the answer to the first question.

Leeann was created to fulfill a specific purpose, including:

1. Donna writes historical and contemporary, and she didn't want readers confused when they picked up one of her books as to which genre to expect.

2. Schlachter is pretty far down the alphabet, and most people who look for books in stores or libraries tend to start at A and work their way to Z. Betts is much closer to the beginning of the alphabet.

3. Donna wanted to experiment with voice and story-telling style, and felt that might be better accomplished through a pen name.

4. Donna wanted to honor her mother and mother-in-law, so here's how she did it: Lee is her husband Patrick's middle name; Ann is her mother-in-law's name; and Betts was her mother's nickname in nursing school.

You will have your own reasons for creating a pseudonym. The most common reasons I've read about are: the desire for anonymity, the multi-genre issue, the new creation in Christ issue (if you wrote erotica, for example, in your 'before' life); and a desire to be somebody you just aren't.

Takeaway: God knows your name, and you cannot hide from Him. However, you can keep your personal and writing lives separate without breaking any laws, either criminal or moral.

Exercises: If you decide to use a pen name, here are some practical steps to take:
1. Search the internet for the name to see if anybody else famous or infamous is already using the name.
2. Check to see if the website is available.
3. Make sure it fits the genre you are writing in. For example, if you write historical, choosing an 'old-fashioned' name like Emily, Amelia, or Grace might be better than choosing Courtney, Paris, or Whitney.

Credibility in our Lives and in our Writing

Court cases abound where one person alleges another has harmed them in some way, either through slander or liable. Police and criminal laboratories are under scrutiny because test results used to either convict or exonerate were proven to have been conducted in error, possibly negating the results. Patients wait for a life-or-death diagnosis based on biopsies, scans, and blood work. Juries determine the guilt or innocence of defendants based on evidence presented or exculpatory evidence withheld.

And within our personal relationships, marriages rise and fall on trust. People are hired and fired based on reputation. Friendships grow or die based on gossip.

Credibility is a really big thing.

If we don't have credibility in our lives, people soon learn not to trust us. If we don't do what we say we're going to do, our family learns not to depend on us. And if we do things we said we weren't going to do, they can't hear what we're telling them because our actions are speaking too loud.

In the same way, we must have credibility in our writing. This starts with the promise we make to our readers: this is a book you're going to be glad you bought. You don't want a reader to say, "I'm glad I borrowed that book. Imagine how bad I'd have felt if I paid for it."

Readers are glad to buy a book that meets their requirements: to entertain; to educate; to edify.

As writers of Christian books, however, we must look to our reason for writing first: to point people to God.

I'm not talking about salvation scenes and all the dirty rotten scoundrels coming to Christ. We must reveal something about God to our readers that perhaps they didn't know. Or didn't realize they knew. Some aspect of His character, His good plans for them, His love for them, His grace and mercy, His love for justice, His compassion.

Then we must fulfill the promise that we know what we're talking about. No matter whether we write historical or contemporary, we must know our characters, our setting, and the details of people living and working in that setting and time period.

Takeaway: To write credibly, we must trust that our reader is intelligent enough to 'get the story'.

Exercises:
1. Check your manuscript for repetitions of why the hero and heroine shouldn't get together. Do not repeat the reason they shouldn't get together more than about four times throughout the entire story. Your reader will get it.
2. Check your manuscript to make sure references to specifics such as car models, modern conveniences, historical events, and the like is correct. The fastest way to lose readers' confidence is to make a dumb mistake.
3. Make sure your story lines up with the genre, the title, and the back cover copy. Don't disappoint readers by promising one thing and delivering another.

Ghostwriting by any other name

What do ghostwriting, work-for-hire, contract writer have in common? They are all different names for the same process—someone wants a book written and they don't want to spend the time writing it themselves, so they hire someone—the Writer—to do the work.

My first work-for-hire was through a contact at a writer's conference. While he wasn't interested in the devotional book I was proposing, he liked the samples I provided. He was a book packager, and he needed a Writer for a project for a publisher.

My second work-for-hire was through the same book packager, who, because of our previous experience, wanted me to write a book in a series for another publisher.

In both cases, the book packager had specifications from the publisher, including the length of each devotional or chapter, Bible versions, layout requirements for each devotional or chapter, and so on. The total contract was broken down into due dates and payments for timely submissions, as well as turnaround times on editing feedback.

My three ghostwriting projects were from various sources and referrals. In one case, the Author had an idea and I came up with the book title, table of contents for each chapter, and wrote each chapter from scratch. In the other two cases, the Authors had a rough draft of the book and an idea of the story they wanted to tell, and I took their draft, edited and organized it, added images they provided, and added creative non-fiction story telling techniques to make the book more readable. In one case, I designed a cover as well.

For me, I have to care about the project before I am willing to invest up to six months in the book. And I also must be willing to work with the person, to set boundaries for what I will and won't do, and commit to being the lead in the project.

Here are some suggestions:

1. Always make a contract. Spell out what you will do, what you expect of the Author, schedules, cancellation options, and how you will communicate.

2. Build in a little wiggle room for life.
3. Leave time in your schedule for your own writing.
4. Be honest and upfront regarding what you will write and what you won't.
5. Be willing to broach the subject of more money if the Author tries to add in services not included in the original contract.
6. If you get into the project then realize it isn't for you, be willing to quit.
7. Offer a payment plan. If the Author wants to pay up front, I usually offer a 10% discount on the total.
8. Get payment before the work is done. If the Author cancels the project, they don't owe you any money and you aren't left scrambling to get money from a disgruntled Author.

If you would like to see my sample ghostwriting contract, type in https://historythrutheages.wordpress.com/ghostwriting/ then click on the link to the sample contract.

Takeaway: You don't need a university degree to be a ghostwriter.

Exercises:
1. Make a list of the kinds of books you enjoy reading. You might also enjoy writing a book like one of these for someone else.
2. Look online for clients who seek someone else to write their book for them.
3. Tell folks you're a ghostwriter; put it on your business card, your website, and mention it in your newsletter and email signature.

Ghostwriting isn't a mystery

Ghostwriting, or writing for somebody else where it will appear as if THEY wrote the article or book, isn't something new. You can go back to the Bible and find instances where the Apostle Paul had someone else write his letters for him. He dictated, they wrote. Ghostwriting is much the same.

The Author, whose name will be on the cover, usually has an idea of what they want, some notes and research, a story, maybe an outline, some chapters written, a defined market for the book, and maybe even a publisher.

The Writer (that's you), brings a combination of experience, ability, excitement about the project, the time and energy to complete the writing, some ideas about how to finish, and, in some cases, advice on how to format, publish, and market the writing.

In essence, you are selling your work to someone else to use as their own.

Wait a minute. That's plagiarism, isn't it? No. Because you are selling the work to them. It's like a (gulp) job. If you worked for a company that builds houses, their name is on the house, not yours, because they paid you to do it.

Doesn't ghostwriting steal your creativity? I would hasten to say no; it feeds creativity because it provides an outlet, it provides the opportunity to learn as we work, and it provides the resources necessary to fund our own personal projects.

Some writers say they don't want anything published that doesn't have their name on it. The Apostle Paul, who wrote two-thirds of the New Testament, doesn't have one book named after him. Be honest: seeing your name on the cover of a book fills your heart with pride. Are we writing for the glory of God, or for our own pride? If we're writing for God's glory, then it won't matter whose name is on the cover.

Ghostwriting is a great way to generate income when you're between projects. You can hone your writing skills, particularly if you're asked to complete a project that is outside what you usually write. The process can develop strong friendships with the Author as you work together, often hearing intimate details about someone else's life. It's a good way to put you in your right place: as transcriber of God's stories.

Ghostwriting projects abound. You can find them through groups and organizations such as The Christian Pen, through online writing groups, publishers, and through personal referrals. Let folks know you're open to ghostwriting, keep improving your writing skills, and allow God to drop that perfect project into your lap.

Always have a contract that spells out the details and contingencies of your agreement. Expect to spend some time talking with the Author, and build in time for research. Follow through and complete the assignment ahead of time as much as is it in your power to do. If you would like a sample contract, click on the Ghostwriting tab on my blog.

Takeaway: Many people earn a good living writing for others. Consider it a ministry.

Exercises:
1. Make a list of topics you can write credibly about.
2. Decide how much time per week, per month, or per year you can give to ghostwriting without neglecting your own projects.
3. Look up websites and blogs of other ghostwriters. Contact them and let them know you're available. Perhaps they have too much work or a project they don't think is a good fit for them that you could take on.

Holding it all together

Running any kind of business out of the home is never easy. There always seem to be so many potential distractions, including well-meaning friends who think that because you are at home means you're available; spouses who see no problem with you running errands during the work day; children who expect you at their beck and call, particularly in the summer; and a mountain of household chores that call from nooks and crannies.

But I'm preaching to the choir.

We all know the problems. Now, what are some solutions?

Over the years, I've found the following 5 items to be mandatory to maintaining my schedule, my professionalism, and my sanity.

1. A good calendar: to keep all my projects and appointments organized. I used to be exclusively paper, before I had any technology that enabled me to go beyond the calendar on my desk. One year I used one of those large blotter-type calendars, but soon found that was inconvenient to take with, so the next year I switched to a book type, two pages per month, that laid flat on my desk. But I struggled to take that one with me. So last year I upgraded my cell phone and am now using that calendar exclusively, except I still have a paper one on my desk where I track my blog activity and other in-office things, such as newsletter dates and birthdays. I only take the paper calendar with me when I travel, because otherwise I'm in the office every day and can check if there's something I need to attend to. In my cell phone calendar, which I also sync with my husband's cell phone and my tablet, I color code each activity. Coordinating calendars is imperative, and you and whoever you coordinate with should make a commitment not to add anything without checking the calendar first. You might prefer an online calendar such as Google calendar: https://calendar.google.com/calendar or Windows Calendar: http://www.wincalendar.com/desktop-calendar . There are plenty of online choices.

2. A digital filing system: Since I'm old school, I learned to create and use paper filing systems, and honestly, my digital filing system closely mimics a paper system. I create a major "filing cabinet",

such as Business, then I create subfolders that I treat like "drawers", such as "Writing", "Accounting Stuff", "Government Stuff", and so on. In each "drawer", I then create subfolders that are like "sections". So in the "Writing Drawer", I have "Editing Clients", "Non-Fiction", "Fiction" sections, for example. And so on, down to the final folder with the piece of information I am saving. I store all of this in a section of my computer called "My Files". There is only data in this section. No downloaded files. No programs. Nothing with an .exe extension that could interfere with my data files. Software should be installed in "Program" folders, and any programs you download from the internet should be stored in "Downloaded Program" folders, all kept separate, so there is less chance of one corrupting the other.

    3.   A backup system: I back up "My Files" on a regular basis. In reality, these are the only files that are changed on a regular basis. Program files are either on disk or accessible online, so you don't need to keep backing them up.

    4.   An external drive for Photos: If you're anything like me, I take thousands of pictures. To keep them safe and not clutter up--and therefore slow down--your computer, I store mine on an external hard drive. I sort them into folders by their subject matter, then into subfolders by their location. For example, I have a folder called "old houses and mansions", and in that folder, subfolders such as "Avery House", "Harvey House", and so on. In the "Avery House" folder, I have several folders because I've been there a couple of times.

    5.   A Deadline White Board: I keep this propped up on my desk, and I make notes of things I specifically need to do today and this week, with an estimated time to complete. Here is a picture of a recent board. I can add, cross off, erase when done, change the due date when necessary, leave an item there to deal with later, such as with an editing client who I've sent work back to and am waiting for their next installment. And the coolest thing of all is I can take a picture of the board when I'm going to be out of the office for a few hours or days, and I have my To Do list with me.

Takeaway: Whatever we relegate to a calendar or a list doesn't have to float around in our heads all day.

Exercises:
1. Prioritize what you need to do today and focus on doing the most important.

2. Start with prayer and quiet time. If you're too busy for that, you're too busy.
3. Anything you don't get done today either wasn't as important as you thought, or didn't have to be done today. Consider setting it at least two days out on your calendar.

Hosting a Successful Book Event

Regardless of whether you already have a published book in your hand or you're still working on your project, you can host or participate in a successful book event.

From my experience, there are several kinds of events:

1. Book signing—usually held in a bookstore, these events focus on the author promoting and selling their books. The bookstore generally directs these events, including the placement of the author in the store and how the books are displayed, usually on a table.

2. Facebook Hop—choose a theme, line up some authors, and promote the event everywhere. When authors offer a prize for a comment left on their FB Author Page, that seems to draw in participants. Each author posts the same "blurb", and includes the link to the first stop on the hop, as well as the next stop following them. Visitors are encouraged to check out their blog, subscribe to newsletters, etc. This is a great way to build a following and to increase your email list.

3. Book Promotion—this event focuses on the books, not the authors, although book sales and author signings are often included. Can be held in a bookstore, although works well at festivals and fairs, community centers, writing conferences, and other venues. The key here is: who will attend? Then simply schedule activities around that demographic. For example, if your main audience will be readers, give away books as prizes; come up with book-related questions for a game of Trivial Pursuit; have a scavenger hunt with book-related answers. Plan to include light refreshments, and mention this in your social media posts. Nothing draws a crowd like free food. Keep it simply—ice water, sparkling water/non-alcoholic 'wine', meat and cheese rollups, fruit, small sandwiches, bite-size cookies—it doesn't have to be elaborate.

There are as many kinds of book events as there are books, I'm sure, but here are my top tips to hosting a successful event:

a. Choose a venue, including date and time: for this, you'll want to decide what your goal is. If you simply want to sell books, a bookstore might be a good choice. If you want to promote more than just locally, a Facebook Hop would be ideal. Want a party? A local book event is the ticket.

    b.   Invite other authors to participate: Good sources are your writing friends and writing groups you belong to. Tell them to invite authors they know. The more the merrier, and the more authors involved, the more promotion, the busier the event will look, and the more people get invited.

    c.   For a physical venue, visit and see what the layout is, what furniture (including table and chairs) is available, and whether food is allowed (if you're planning food).

    d.   Books: if you are traditionally published, make sure the venue has the information it needs to order books. If you are independently published, make sure you have enough books on hand. You don't want to run out!

    e.   Cross-promotion: if you don't have a newsletter, now is a good time to promise yourself you'll do that. Have participants fill out their information, including name, phone number (to contact them if they win the free book you're going to give them for signing up), and email address. Make sure there is a disclaimer that says you won't share their information and they can unsubscribe any time. Then go into MailChimp or some other Email Subscription Service, and set up an account for your first newsletter.

    f.   Readings: readers love to hear snippets of books they might like to buy, so arrange a schedule for each author to read a scene or a short story. Keep it to 5 minutes or less for each author, and break up the readings by putting a drawing or a game in between every two readings, just so folks can get up and move around a bit.

    g.   Giveaways: Besides offering free books to winners of drawings, also have bookmarks, pens, whatever other promotional items you like. If you are holding the event in a bookstore, think about holding a drawing for anybody who buys something other than your book from the store to encourage folks to purchase from your host.

Takeaway: The most successful events are planned well in advance. Very little good comes of leaving the details to the last minute.

Exercises:
1. Decide what kind of an event you want. In-person or online?

2. For a bookstore signing, consider asking 2-4 other authors who write in your genre to join you. You'll draw a bigger crowd.
3. For an online event, consider getting 6-9 other authors, choose a theme, and pick a date. Make sure you promote it.

Judging a Writing Contest

Entering writing contests can be nerve-wracking as you wait for results, but oh, so exhilarating when you learn you did well or even won! Congratulations to you if you've had a good experience.

But for every winner, there are dozens, if not hundreds, of other authors who didn't win. To you I say good for you for being bold enough to put your work out there.

And for every writing contest, there are dozens, if not hundreds, of judges who most often donate their time to read, comment on, and score the entries. To you I say thank you for your service.

Judging a writing contest can be almost as nerve-wracking as entering. We must constantly remind ourselves that this is another author's work and words, a story close to their heart, one they invested many hours to produce. And just like the Golden Rule says, we must always strive to treat every entrant the way we want to be treated.

Writing contests usually go begging for judges because most writers think that if they aren't multi-published or haven't won multiple contests, they have nothing to add, but this is simply not true. A good judge is one who can be impartial, one who knows the rules and recognizes when they're being broken, is willing to let the rules be broken if it serves a good purpose in the story, and will commit to returning the entries on time.

Contests differ in their requirements. For example, a contest for newer writers usually includes the first five or so pages. More advanced contests could be up to about 20 pages, and contests for published works usually require the judge to read the whole book. Score sheets are provided with a list of questions about opening lines, characterization, plot, dialogue, and the mechanics such as POV and punctuation.

If you like to read, if you enjoy providing feedback, and if you can stick to a deadline and meet it, no matter what else comes up-- because, it will--then you'd make a good contest judge. Keep your eyes open, and when you see a contest that you wish you had an entry for but don't, contact them and ask if they need judges. Some contests will allow you to judge even if you have an entry in the contest; you usually won't be permitted to judge in the category you entered in.

A good place to start is with ACFW. While the contests are closed for this season, First Impressions will open again in September. Here is the contact information:

ACFW First Impressions Contest impress@acfw.com
Florida Tapestry Awards Kristen Stieffel kristen@kristenstieffel.com
ACFW Genesis Contest Betsy St Amant betsystamant@yahoo.com
Daphne DuMaurier RWA contest Janie Crouch janiecrouch@verizon.net
ACFW Carol Awards carolawards@acfw.com
Rattler Contest Leola Ogle jeffleola@yahoo.com

Takeaway: You don't need to be a published author to judge in a contest.

Exercises:
1. Decide what kind of books you like to read and look for contests with those categories.
2. Introduce yourself, focusing on your passion for books, for encouraging new authors, instead of your lack of experience.
3. Pray that the Lord would bring the entries to you that will use your skills to help these new authors.

Online Courses

Busy, busy. Everybody is busy. And if your life is anything like mine, I don't have time to sleep, let alone take another writing course.

But recently I've discovered a way to learn from the comfort of my home: online writing courses.

For me, online courses have solved several problems:

1. Not enough evenings in the week to go to a class
2. Save the travel time.
3. I'm an introvert and don't really want to be around a bunch of people.
4. I am badge-oriented, love taking tests, love acing said tests, which makes people less committed to course very uneasy.
5. I don't do well in situations where I'm surrounded by people who don't share the same--or at least a similar--worldview.

All that said, and I don't know exactly how it happened, but I'm on a number of mailing lists of folks who offer online courses that range from free to several hundred dollars. The links follow, but here are a few things to keep in mind:

1. Don't overextend yourself--be realistic about how much time you're willing to invest, how much time the course will take, and how much work are you willing to put in?
2. Consider the cost--not just the money, but the time taken from whatever else you would have done. If you'd have spent that time earning an income, that's also part of the course.
3. The relevance of the material--as you take more courses, you'll get more offers, and sometimes the course offered will be way out in left field from where you started. Ask yourself: will this course make me a better person/better writer/better editor or whatever you're trying to accomplish.
4. Is there a better way to get this same information? For example, instead of taking a 6-week class, maybe you could get the same information from a book.
5. Topics covered--have you seen or heard the same material before and don't really need a full course?
6. Your self-discipline--some courses will spend the last 15 minutes trying to sell you their complete, super-duper course. Can you

say no to that and not be angst-ridden for weeks? If not, skip this course.

I have taken a number of the following courses and had good experiences with all of them. However, before you choose a course, make sure you know why you're taking it.

www.Authoraudience.com by Shelley Hitz has a good range of courses to fit all needs and budgets. She offers many free webinars and podcasts, as well. Plus, Shelly is a believer, which is a bonus, at least in my books.

www.DIYAuthor.com by Chris Well offers lots of free and low-priced courses and webinars, including email courses.

www.FutureLearn.com offers free university quality courses. I've done several of these on forensics, crime scene investigation, psychology, antiquities, and am currently doing one on genealogy research and another on forensic psychology.

www.MaryBuckham.com offers a number of courses which I've purchased, including one on Hooks.

www.Udemy.com has some good podcasts and webinars

www.Teachable.com

www.SellingForAuthors.com by Bryan Cohen has some good stuff.

www.SellMoreBooks.com

www.AuthorMarketingInstitute.com

Takeaway: Even courses designed to save us time and energy can sap our time and energy. Be wise when you invest in an online course.

Exercises:
1. Do some research into what you'd like to learn about.
2. Choose an online service that offers that course and sign up.
3. Set aside the time to effective participate. Don't set yourself up to fail or quit. Take it just as seriously as if it was an in-class course and you had to write a final exam.

These are a Few of my Favorite Things

Sometimes it can be hard for family and friends to come up with a gift idea for us, so having a list of suggestions on hand to fit any budget will relieve their stress and ensure you get something useful.

There are a plethora of writerly tools that will help overcome hurdles little and big in your writing career. Tools are used in every profession. Can you imagine your landscaper coming to mow your lawn without a mower? Maybe all he can afford is a pair of scissors. Would you take him seriously? Or how about if your stylist asked you to bring a cape and a hair dryer because she didn't have one?

If you want to be taken seriously as a writer, you need tools. And they don't have to cost a fortune, either. Following is a list of my favorite writers' tools.

1. At least one good writers conference a year -- depending on your genre and your journey along the writing path, this could be a one-day local seminar, or it could be a three- or four-day intense multi-track conference, or anything in between. A good place to find out about conferences is your writing friends, local writing groups, writing organizations you belong to, and a site I like: www.ShawGuides.com Put "writers conferences" in the search box. You can sort by date, state, or look up by keyword.

2. At least one writers organization -- there are many to choose from. For Christian fiction writers, I recommend American Christian Fiction Writers (www.acfw.com). There are also genre-specific groups for romance, suspense, mystery, sci-fi, and many more. Most large groups have an internet presence, as well as a newsletter/magazine of some sort, contests, continuing education throughout the year, critique groups, and offer reduced rates at conferences for members.

3. A local writers group -- gets you face to face with your writing friends. Can be a chapter of a national organization, although there are plenty of great independent groups. And participate--offer your expertise in other areas such as a position on their operating board, as hostess, or help to

coordinate an event.

4. A critique group -- online or local, doesn't matter. Gives you the chance to learn, to read outside your genre, and to give back.

5. A white board -- I use this one to write down the things I have to do each week. I used to keep my list on paper, but it was discouraging every week to bring forward the things I didn't get done onto a new sheet, plus I was always losing my paper in the pile of stuff on my desk. Some writers like to use a white board to outline a novel, or keep notes about characters. I haven't gotten to that point. But I can keep my To Do list front and center, and I love crossing things off the list. When my husband says, "can you help me with ____", I add it to the list. And I make a note of how long I think it's going to take so I can decide if I want to start a longer project earlier in the day.

The great news about all of these tools is that you can add them to your gift wish list, and let somebody 'surprise' you with something you can use, instead of another pair of fuzzy slippers that look like Elmo.

Although, if someone has a pair that looks like Garfield, I'll trade you a flannel nightgown for them. ☺

Takeaway: There is nothing wrong in receiving (or giving) a practical gift.

Exercises:
1. Make a list of all the things you wish you had that would make your writing life easier.
2. Look for opportunities to give hints.
3. Maybe several members of your family would combine their resources to buy you one of the bigger gifts, such as a conference or a new laptop.

Rejection and Reality

If you love rejection, writing is the job for you.

If you love reality, perhaps you'd best avoid this career choice.

And yet rejection and reality are key to being a successful writer.

So let me share a story that really did happen to me several years ago. I used a post office box for business purposes, and the post office was about four blocks from where we lived. Since it was so close, we used checking the mail as an excuse to take a walk.

On this particular day, which was a Wednesday, I wasn't looking forward to going to the mail. I'd made this same walk on Monday and Tuesday, and the results weren't the happy dance of acceptance.

I was feeling extremely rejected.

Now, you've probably never been there. You're probably one of those writers whose first piece was accepted, serialized, and you're now in syndication.

But not me.

So I said to my hubby, "I don't know if I can face one more rejection letter. It's only Wednesday, and already this week I've had fourteen rejections."

He stopped walking, which made me stop, too, and when I looked up at him, he said, "Do you know how many writers would like to say they have fourteen query letters out there?"

I hadn't thought about it in exactly that way before. All I knew was I seemed to keep pushing out the pieces, and nothing was working. I felt like Julie in the *Julie and Julia* movie of 2009: "Is anybody out there?"

But I knew he was right. And although I resist admitting that, at least to his face, I said, "Right."

Then he said, "If you knew right now that you were never going to publish one word, would you stop writing?"

Asking me that was like asking me if I could stop breathing. Or eating chocolate. Or do long division in my head. Of course the answer was a resounding no!

I shook my head. "I couldn't. The words are in there and they have to come out."

"Then it doesn't matter how many rejections you get."

He was so right. For the second time that day. And the last thing I was going to do was tell him that.

The reality of writing is that you will get rejections. You'll get bad reviews. You'll have editors who say your stuff is horrendous—yes, I had that said about something I'd written. It probably was, but this editor could probably have used a nicer word.

Don't let the fear of rejection keep you from doing what you love. Be willing to learn how to write well, how to prove the naysayers wrong. After all, success is the best revenge!

Takeaway: Rejections and bad reviews don't tell the truth about you. Only God knows that truth.

Exercises:
1. If your writing has never been rejected, you're not submitting enough. Send something out on submission today.
2. If a particular project has been rejected a number of times, take a look at it to see if you're getting similar messages. Maybe you need to revise in some way.
3. Consider hiring a professional editor.

Unlocking the Doors

Do you sometimes feel, in trying to get your book published, that you're rattling at one locked door after another? Perhaps you're struggling to find an agent, or maybe you've been submitting directly to publishers and gotten nothing except rejections. Or worse, silence.

It's okay. We've all been there. Some of us are still there. And we understand that while we trust God to open doors that nobody else can close, and to close doors that we aren't to go through, we also know that when the door is open, we have to walk through. God won't drag us kicking and screaming. He's too much of a gentleman for that.

So what are we to do? Following are three things to focus on as you go through this process of unlocking the doors to publication:

1. Pray. Seriously. Seek the Lord as to His direction for you. Perhaps He has a better plan for you right now. Maybe He's holding back on publication because He knows that's not the best thing for you. I believe He delayed my publication path because He knew that I am an all-or-nothing kind of person: if I got a contract, life in our household would have to stop while I pursued and completed that project. And He had more important things for us to do during that time, including leadership in an international ministry.

2. Pause. If you're anything like me, publication has been a main focus for your books, and anything else is second-best. I had to take a step back and ask myself why I wanted to publish a book. Was it to see my name on the cover? To show somebody I had what it took to be a writer? For fame and money? My first book, a devotional, was done as a work-for-hire project and my name wasn't on the cover. It was in teensy-weensy little print on the inside. Talk about humbling. But this experience made me step back and ask why I wanted to publish. Which brings me to number three.

3. Praise. Yes, you read that right. Praise God for the gift he's given you to string together words into stories that touch lives. Praise Him that He is writing the most important story in you right now, long before the written word gets on to the page. Praise Him that He would choose you to be the first person to hear this story. And Praise Him for using you to reach a lost world.

I truly believe that when we put our writing in the proper place in our lives—never above God, never above our spouse or family—then He will honor this calling to write and will reward our obedience. Your publishing path might be traditional or independent; it might be paper or digital; it might be full-time or part-time, but the important thing is that your path leads you—and others—to know more intimately the God of Words. He is the Word, and He has placed that Word in you to give to others.

Takeaway: Go ahead, unlock some doors. You have the keys you need.

Exercises:
1. If you're struggling on the publishing path, be willing to make some changes to your process, including professional editing, professional manuscript analysis, and joining a critique group.
2. Attend a writer's conference to make connections with authors, editors, and agents, and to learn the craft of writing.
3. Read as many books as you can on the craft of writing.

Why Guest Blog?

If you belong to even one online writers' group, you may already have an invaluable resource right at your fingertips, a veritable gold mine for your blog.

Members of that online group.

Sure, your readers come to your blog to hear from you. But if they are like most readers, they also read other authors.

Gasp!

I know, that news is difficult to bear.

But as authors, bear it we must.

And hosting another author on your blog is a gracious way to accomplish two things: you give your readers the opportunity to learn about other books and authors. And you have the opportunity to draw other readers to your blog.

Wait a minute. Draw other readers to your blog? What a novel idea--pardon the pun.

Your guest blogger has their own circle of followers that you don't have access to. And when your guest appears on your blog, they will let their followers know where they are visiting for that day.

And some of these followers may choose to become your followers.

As I said before, what a novel idea. This time, pun intended.

That is one of the beauties of social media--while we all have our own circle of friends and followers, we can sometimes enjoy the experience of interacting with followers from others' circles.

And like a good hostess who is invited to dinner at someone else's house, your guest may well invite you to be a guest on their blog. Which allows your followers to visit someone else, get to know another author and their books, and then start following them.

And like any good relationship, having more friends doesn't diminish how you feel about your followers, or how they feel about you.

Takeaway: Hosting other authors on your blog is a win-win situation—for them and for you.

Exercises:
1. If you've guest blogged for others in the past, contact them and ask to be scheduled in again.
2. If you've hosted other authors before, contact them and arrange a reciprocal appearance on each other's blogs.
3. Check online groups you belong to and offer to host in exchange for being hosted.

Self-Imposed Deadlines

There is something intimidating about deadlines. When you first sign that contract or make that agreement to have your book in your publisher's hands six months from now, that seems like a long time. Sure, you can take a week off and celebrate. And another week to do some research. Then one of the kids gets the mumps. And another.

And before you know it, it's April 2nd and your book is due April 25th.

What do you do? Panic!

But what about if you're not under an official contract? You don't have a publisher breathing down your neck, waiting for your book. You have all the time in the world, right?

No. You don't.

If you are a writer, then you must write. And if you're a writer, you must be writing for someone other than yourself. At the very least, as a Christian writer, you are writing for God. And even if He is the only One who ever sees what you're writing, He has an expectation that at some point, you'll be ready to move on to the next project.

Failing to set a finish date sets you up to fail.

So even if you're not under someone else's deadline, you should be under one of your own.

How can you stick to that date?

1. Make up some business cards with the cover on it and the release date.
2. Tell other people.
3. Spread the news on social media.
4. Write it on a calendar in ink.
5. Keep a picture of the cover in front of you with the release date written on it.
6. Schedule time to accomplish the work by the date you say.

What happens when life gets in the way?

You might need to put aside something else in your life so you can meet your personal deadline. That's right.

- Get up 30 minutes earlier.
- Go to bed 30 minutes later.
- Skip your lunch hour and write.
- Skip television one or two or three nights a week.
- Take your laptop when you go to an appointment and work while you're waiting.
- Tell your family what your goal is, and ask them to help you meet that goal

Self-Imposed deadlines might not be about finishing a book. Maybe you've spent way too much time on research but you can't tear yourself away. So set a deadline. Two more days and then you're done. You might be pleasantly surprised at how much you get done in the next two days.

Maybe you're spending too much time re-writing. Face it--ten years is too long. One year is probably too long. Repeat after me: it will never be perfect.

And that's because you are learning as you go. You will continue to learn. You want to put out the best product possible, but not getting the book done isn't going to help anybody. Let it go. Or pay someone else to re-write for you.

Takeaway: Practice setting deadlines so when you get a publishing contract, you'll be used to writing to a schedule.

Exercises:
1. Set a goal for your current writing project. Maybe it's words per day, chapters per week, or finish the first draft by the end of this month.
2. Next month, raise the bar.
3. If you miss the deadline, review your goal and what happened. Maybe it was unrealistic, or maybe you weren't committed.

Writing Contest Do's and Don'ts

So you read about the latest contest, you snag a file from one of your computer folders, attach it, pay the entry fee, and sit back, waiting for THE CALL. Because, after all, this is the best thing you've ever written—at least, that's what your mother said three years ago when you showed it to her.

And then you get the news: you didn't even final, let alone win. And the judges' comment attached confirmed what you knew all along: the contest was a scam. These people just don't get your writing style. They know nothing.

Or do they?

Writing contests are about as different as cats. Sure, all cats have claws and whiskers and they meow, but not all cats are the same. Some like to cuddle. Some like to romp. And some just don't care whether you're dead or alive so long as you feed them.

Writing contests are the same: some make you feel warm and fuzzy; some challenge you to do better; and some are only in it for the money.

How do we wade through the mire? Here's a short and by no means exhaustive list of things to look for in a writing contest, as well as a list of suggestions for succeeding in contests.

Choosing a Contest:

1. What are you hoping to get out of it? Do you hope to win the grand prize, or simply get some feedback on the first 15 pages before you spend the next year writing the book?

2. If you want to win the grand prize, read the instructions that come with every contest. Sometimes cleverly disguised as Rules, these parameters tell you how to get past the gatekeeper.

3. Does this group hold more than one contest per year? If so, that might be their only business. Beware.

4. Does this contest promise publication to the winner? If so, beware. Nobody should guarantee publication because even a winner can be really badly written.

5. If the contest publishes a list of past winners, check them out. Are the authors now published? And is it with a traditional publisher or a vanity press? Many contests turn into tough sales pitches for every entrant, asking thousands of dollars for editing, cover design, book formatting, and the like.

6. Does your story really fit the genre? If you choose a category, make sure you choose wisely. Judges who read sci-fi simply won't get your chick-lit book simply because you thought the competition might be less there.

7. Have you done more than pull out an old file and send it off? Read through, polish, edit, revise before hitting SEND. If you've lived more than fifteen minutes since you first wrote it, you've learned something about the craft of writing.

8. Do you recognize the names of any of the judges? Can you search for them online? Do they all work for the same company? Beware.

9. How does the scoring work? If there are three judges and all scores are included, you might end up with a lower score than if the lowest one is dropped and the other two averaged. Sometimes judges just don't "get" the story, and that's okay. Not all readers will "get" it, either. You shouldn't be penalized because one out of three was having a bad day, or got buttonholed into judging sci-fi when they really like Amish mysteries.

10. Will you receive written feedback either in the form of judges' comments or an evaluation sheet? This is sometimes worth more than the grand prize. Contests that seek to improve your writing are always the best place to invest your money and time.

<u>Succeeding in a Contest</u>
1. Read the rules.
2. Follow the rules EXACTLY. If the rules say 1/4 inch margin and quadruple spaced, do it. You don't have to like it. They make the rules. They will judge your work based on your ability to follow instructions. Some of the judges might be editors, and they want to weed out writers who won't do as they're asked.
3. Choose your genre carefully. (See #6 above) Don't expect the coordinator to read your submission and move it to the proper genre.
4. Check out the contest online first. There are several good places to check out contest scams, including:

https://www.wikihow.com/Avoid-Writing-Contest-Scams
http://writing-world.com/contests/scams.shtml
https://thewritelife.com/writing-contests/

5. Choose a contest associated with a conference you're planning on attending. These are usually legitimate, and more likely to fit into your genre since you're going there for a reason.

6. Choose a contest associated with a writing organization you're already a member of. Same reasoning as #5.

7. Ask around for others' experiences about contests they entered.

8. Consider the entry fee and whether it's equitable for the potential win. A $15 entry fee with feedback for a $100 prize may sound high, but it's a good deal for the feedback. A $45 entry fee where 10,000 authors entered last year is a good money-making effort with little chance of winning.

9. Consider where you are in your writing career. If you're already published, contest opportunities are much fewer, and unless the contest is something really specific, such as Best of Arizona Military Fiction, you might be better off skipping it. If you're pre-published, a win is a nice kudo in your bio and could attract an agent or an editor.

Whatever you decide about entering a contest or not, the real secret to success in writing is to keep reading. Keep writing. Look for ways to give back.

And if you win, invest the money back into your writing before you plan a vacation or a cruise or buy a new car. Unless, of course, your next book requires that kind of research (smile).

Takeaway: You can win a contest—if you follow the rules.

Writing on a Deadline

Just when you think things can't get any busier, they do—you have a deadline to produce a certain number of words by a certain date. Maybe you're under contract for a book. Maybe it's a magazine article, a devotional, or even a simple blog post like this one.

And yet that date looms like a guillotine over your head.

You sit at the computer and will the words to come. But they won't.

Maybe if you watched some television, that might get the creative juices flowing. But it doesn't.

Perhaps a walk around the block. An hour later you limp home after twisting an ankle stepping off the curb. Ice the swelling. Then heat. Then a nap. Then –

Wait a minute. What about that deadline?

Back to the computer. Sit in the chair. Stare at the screen.

Nothing.

Now what?

Now is the time to do what you should have done the first time you sat down.

Pray.

Yes, you read that correctly.

Pray.

This is my favorite version: *Lord, give me ears to hear the words You dictate. Let me transcribe this story/blog article/devotional/poem for You. And thank You for letting me be the first person to hear these words. May Your words change me first, and then change others. Amen.*

Not only is this prayer on target, it also reminds me Who is the boss. This prayer humbles me to my rightful position. And being a transcriber is Biblical. Even the Apostle Paul says he had scribes who wrote for him.

That's our job. That's our goal. Write the only story worth telling, from the One who is the creator of story.

And by the way, once I have my priorities right, it's not a deadline; it's a lifeline.

Takeaway: You can choose a deadline to a lifeline by putting God in control.

Exercises:
1. Identify those things that distract you from writing.
2. Identify those situations that create fear of failure.
3. Lay these two lists before the Cross.

Writing Through the Summer – or any season

The summer/Christmas/harvest time/whatever the distraction is well upon us, and there are many activities and opportunities calling to us. Regardless of the what—kids home from school, family and friends visiting, vacations to plan and enjoy—we struggle to find the time to write?

Here's the ugly truth: we won't.

But all is not lost: we can MAKE time to write.

Here are some suggestions:

- Set your clock for 15 or 30 minutes earlier to get up in the morning. The days are warm, the sun will likely already be up, so it's not nearly as difficult as it would be during the winter months.
- Bring a notepad and pen wherever you go, including the beach, the park, the neighborhood pool, the grocery store, the library. Jot down some ideas, snatches of conversation you overhear at the checkout, character descriptions you might use.
- Use every activity as an opportunity for research. Just because you don't write historicals doesn't mean you don't need to research. Taking the kids for swimming lessons? Ask the swim coach what training she needs to do this job. Dropping the kids off at the library for a reading hour? Talk to your librarian about your books and the possibility of doing a reading. Grocery store? Ask the cashier about his unusual name.
- Read as much as you can.
- Watch movies.
- Go to special events such as field days at the local museum, botanic gardens, and zoos.
- When you go on vacation, look for places to see along the way.
- Watch for historic markers along the highway.

Incorporating writing time into your day will keep your story in your mind and make it easier to get back to the actual writing. Plus, if your mind is brimming over with ideas, dialogue, descriptions, and details, the writing will feel as though it's flowing from your fingertips.

Takeaway: If you had a deadline, you would write no matter who came to visit or what holiday was being celebrated.

Split Personality or Writing Under a Pen Name

Leeann, my alter ego, and I were chatting the other day.

She wanted to know why I created her.

"I was writing and hoping to publish in two different genres: historical suspense and contemporary suspense. I didn't want to confuse my readers by writing in different genres."

"How did you pick my name?"

"My husband's middle name is Lee, his mother's middle name is Ann, and my mother's nickname in nursing school was Betts."

"Isn't making up a name illegal?"

"Not unless I'm trying to avoid a legal claim or defraud somebody."

She chewed on her bottom lip, a funny habit she has. "How do you keep us straight?"

I smiled at her. "First of all, you're cute and perky and all the things I'm not. Second, you write different stories than I write."

"Such as?"

"Most of my historical suspense are stories about women who have made some bad choices, and now they want to straighten out their lives. Your stories are about stronger, quirkier women who are driven to excel."

"Sounds like you."

Now it was my turn to chew my bottom lip. Maybe she inherited that trait from me. "But the women you write about don't know they are strong. Or quirky. And the women I write about are just like me. Hoping it's true that God is a God of second chances. And finding out He is."

"So we're different but the same?"

I patted her on the head like she was an obedient puppy. "Exactly."

Takeaway: There is no formula for choosing a pen name.

Exercises:
1. Do some research online about other authors who have used pen names.
2. Do you need a pen name? If so, why?
3. Come up with a character sketch for your alter ego's personality and persona.

The 10-day Writing Challenge

Have you ever stared at a blank computer screen and wondered what on earth you were thinking when you thought you were a writer? Or maybe you've pounded away at the keyboard and cranked out a thousand words, but when you read them, realized they were gibberish and needed to be deleted? Or perhaps you've written a complete novel, or two, or three, but can't seem to find the energy to edit them, or send them to an agent or publisher. Maybe you signed up for NaNoWriMo last month and couldn't even get started.

Writing is hard. It's hard to be rejected. Criticized. Told you have plot holes. Or cardboard characters. Or you need to join a writers group and learn how to write. Or your story line is boring.

I know how you feel. Really, I do. I've been told all of that, and more. "Horrendous" was once used to describe a project I submitted to an editor.

So how do we overcome all of the voices--including our own--telling us we can't do this? How do we get enough oomph in our engine to continue writing until we reach the end of the book? How do we persevere long enough to see success, however we define that for our writing?

A 10-day writing challenge might be the perfect solution to all of these problems. It's short enough not to eat up too much time. Each day's activity takes twenty minutes or less. And by the time you complete Day 10, you'll have character sketches and an outline for a book.

Here we go, the abbreviated version:

Day 1: Set a timer for 3 minutes. Write down why you're taking this challenge. Go ahead, be silly. Be insightful. Be honest.

Day 2: Set a timer for 3 minutes. Write down things you're passionate about. Passion as in you could talk for hours without notes. Passion as in it gets your blood boiling when you hear someone else say it's not important.

Day 3: Set a timer for 3 minutes. Write down things you're good at. Not expert. Just something you do adequately.

Day 4: Set a timer for 3 minutes. Write down the titles of books you want to write. If you can't think of any, write down the titles of books you wish you'd written.

Day 5: Set a timer for 3 minutes. Choose one title from Day 4. List the characters and the setting.

Day 6: Set a timer for 3 minutes. Write your acceptance speech for an Academy Award for when the novel from Day 5 is turned into a movie.

Day 7: Set a timer for 3 minutes. Write the opening paragraph for the book from Day 6.

Day 8: Set a timer for 3 minutes. Write a two-sentence summary of the book from Day 7. What you'd say in response to the question, "So, what's your book about?"

Day 9: Set a timer for 3 minutes. Write a one-sentence summary of each chapter of the book you worked on in Days 5 through 8.

Day 10: Set a timer for 3 minutes. Write the final scene for the book you've been working on in Days 5 through 9.

That's it. From idea to outline in ten days. Now, write that book!

Takeaway: You can produce an outline for your next writing project in ten days.

Encouragement

Hard Tack and Hard Knocks

Most readers of historical fiction have heard of hard tack but may not know what it looks like, tastes like, its origin or its uses.

Hard tack was a mixture of flour, lard, salt, and baking soda that, when baked, was—well, hard. Seagoing ships had a problem with storing fresh bread because it would mold quickly in the damp, warm below-decks environment of the ship's galley (kitchen).

Hard tack was originally served as-is—in small lumps called cakes, about four inches long and two inches thick. Sailors gnawed at the concoction or broke it into pieces and soaked it in their soup or tea to make it more easily eaten.

At some point in history (exact date unknown), somebody came up with the idea of soaking and boiling the hard tack, resulting in a semi-solid mass that, in Newfoundland, became known as brewis, pronounced bruise. By itself, brewis is bland, but when mixed with salt fish or fresh fish and slathered with molasses, becomes a gourmet dish in itself.

A recent release, *The Physics of Love*, is set in Newfoundland, where I was born and spent much of my growing-up years. The story is based on my father's life and circumstances, and recounts his life in a small town during the 1930's and 1940's. Fish and brewis, as the dish is called in Newfoundland, was a staple during that time. Because refrigeration was scarce, salt fish was most often used, with the fish being dried, or cured, on platforms called flakes, which were made of stripped tree branches. Flakes still dot wharves and beaches all around the island.

If you have the opportunity to visit Newfoundland—and a surprising number of people have told me that going there is on their list of places to see—make sure to stop in at a small restaurant and ask for Fish and Brewis, with plenty of molasses. The little square pieces of browned something are called scruncheons, Newfie-talk for fried fatback, a pork product consisting of an inner layer of skin and the next inch or so of fat. Hmmm-mmm good!

Takeaway: Every place has its own history that's unique to it. Look for the history everywhere you go.

Exercises:
1. The next time you visit your hometown, make it a point to talk to the town historian or go to the historical society to learn more about your town's history.
2. Read books and watch movies about places you'd like to visit. Note the difference in dialect, accent, and customs.
3. Sketch an outline for a book you'd like to write about what you've learned from this article and the above exercises.

Hazy But Not Lazy Days

Any dreams I might have had about those lazy, hazy days of summer evaporated weeks ago. I have been on a fast-forward race through an already hot and dry summer, always trying—but never quite succeeding—at catching up.

My original plans included completing a book I started months ago--hasn't happened yet, although I've spent some time thinking about it.

And I was going to spend some hours in my garden.

I've weeded twice, for about five minutes each time. Transplanted two rose bushes because of major water line work. They aren't looking good.

And I wasn't going to work my way through the summer, confined indoors at the computer.

As I said, any dreams I had . . .

So what's a writer to do?

As the saying goes, "When faced with lemons, make lemonade".

I made lemonade from my plans gone awry.

The place to start was to acknowledge I am not the Queen of the Universe. While I might like to think I am, I am not. That was a huge step to take. My plans were not—gulp—the only way to get through the summer.

The next thing was to remember who is the King of the Universe. As a Christian, that's where I should have started my planning. Once I let God take over, and accepted that perhaps His plans are better than mine—I know, there's a verse in the Bible about that—I had a lot more peace.

So when I wanted to stop at a museum on a recent research trip but ran out of time and it closed before I got there, I took a deep breath and looked for another opportunity. And sure enough, the site had great interpretation signs, and I was able to spend more time getting a feel for the ambience of the site.

When I planned to spend the day writing and catching my breath between busy days, but our basement flooded because a contractor left a hose running next to the foundation, instead I had to spend the day going through boxes of wet paper. But in the process, I found three books from my school years that hadn't been damaged and which I now have on my bookshelf. Kind of like reuniting with old friends you haven't seen in a long time.

And take today for instance. I had a vision of writing my guest blogs for the month and getting them sent out. Cross that off the list. Instead I spent time helping a friend find a file she'd worked on for two hours that just zapped itself into that black hole in space computer programs like to tuck our hard work into. But in the process, she learned how to find files that tend to slip away, and I got to experience the joy of helping another.

So as you are plowing your way through the summer, maybe looking forward to getting the kids back into school, or hoping to get some structure into your life again, remember to stop and ask God what He has in store for you today.

I've found it's the best way to stay in control.

Takeaway: Letting God be in control is the best place to be.

Exercises:
1. Check your calendar and cross off at least one thing if you're feeling overwhelmed.
2. Stop and ask God to tell you what He wants you to accomplish today.
3. Do it.

Keep on Keeping on

Do you ever feel like you're writing in a vacuum? Maybe nobody out there is interested in what you have to say? Maybe your mother-in-law/next door neighbor/geeky cousin are right, and nobody wants to read what you've written?

Well, I have news for you: I feel like that often.

And so do many other authors who are way more successful than I am.

Not that I consider myself so successful, particularly when I look at my royalties statement.

So why keep going? Why not give up and spend my time eating chocolates and watching daytime television?

First of all, my hips couldn't take it.

And secondly, because I'd have to choose to be disobedient to God's call on my life.

So maybe that's actually first of all.

And if God has called you to be a writer, or just called you to write one particular book or story or article, then you don't want to say, "Sorry, God, You must be wrong."

A writer isn't a writer because they sell a million books, although that would be nice. A writer writes.

So, if you sit when you don't want to, if you type words into a computer or write words on a blank page or speak words into a recording device, you are a writer.

I've felt like giving up many times. I've written more than a dozen books that are sitting with my agent and looking for new homes, hopefully with a publisher. I've written nearly a dozen more that I've independently published because I felt that was the best niche for them. And still I feel like calling it quits.

I don't because of a 2-inch by 2-inch piece of paper that sits next to my laptop where I can see it.

"My calling is to be a writer who declares God's glory to all the world by drawing people to Christ by the Word, using parables of second chances from our second. . . and third. . . and fourth chance God."

See, I've needed second. . . and third. . . and fourth chances from God many times in my past, for multiple reasons and through numerous situations. And I figure I'm probably not alone.

So, if my stories can touch just one person, help them see the love of Christ through the characters and the plot, then I've done exactly what God called me to do.

He dictates, and I simply transcribe.

That takes the pressure off me for the results. Which frees me to write stories that for some strange reason only I can write.

So figure out why God has called you to write. Then put it where you can see it every time you try to come up with a reason to quit. Use it as your reason not to quit.

Takeaway: Look for reasons to keep on writing, not for reasons to quit.

Exercises:
1. Do you find yourself wanting to quit often? Perhaps there's a pattern. Too much stress from your real job. Family pressures. Seasonal stresses. Write a list.
2. Determine that you won't even think about writing when facing any of the situations in #1.
3. Pray for the Lord to release you from these stresses so you can be obedient to His call on your life.

Knowing the Author

I've recently been revamping my social media, mainly because now I have to do it myself. But this is a good thing, because I'd created a monster that got out of control.

When I sat down and looked at my social media plan, which really was "if it's not working, do more", I realized something very important: I'd completely left God out of my plan. (Thank you, wise husband, for pointing this out to me).

As I prayed about this, a scripture verse came to mind: *The right word spoken at the right time is as beautiful as gold apples in a silver bowl.* (Proverbs 25:11 NCV)

I thought about that for a while, and the Lord spoke to my heart: when you think of Me as Author, what do you want to know about Me?

The answer was easy: I wanted to know God had written the Bible for me. That if nobody else read it, it was still worth writing. I wanted to know that I could learn about God through His book. And that when I meet Him in person, He will be exactly how I pictured Him from His book.

I saw where God was going with this: readers want to know that the author of the book they're reading is real, that the author cares about them as an individual, not just as a cash cow. They want to believe they can get to know me through my books, and that if they meet me at a party and talk to me, they'll say, "You are exactly how I thought you'd be."

When we write authentically, our readers know more about who we are because we are in some of our characters through their worldviews, beliefs, and actions.

When we write authentically, we are writing with one single reader in mind. Our books should point the reader to God first, and then hopefully our stories solve a problem, fill a need, or encourage and entertain. And a really great book, like the one God wrote for you, will do all of these things.

So when readers read my books, I hope they learn that I love numbers almost to the exclusion of everything else; that I trust numbers more than people because numbers never change; that I don't much like to exercise; and that I strive to be a submissive wife to my husband but I still struggle with that.

And maybe they'll also see that I wish I were more like Carly: quicker to jump in to help; quick on the comebacks; and not take myself so seriously.

Because really, in some way, even if it's below the surface, the stories we write should contain some of ourselves.

God's book did.

Takeaway: Writing authentically opens the doors to our readers' emotions.

Exercises:
1. Make a list of the books you want to write over the next year, two years, five years.
2. Pick the first one in the list and write out a short sketch or synopsis.
3. Pick a date to start writing.

No More Name-Dropping

When we spend time with somebody who specializes in name-dropping, we can quickly begin to question ourselves. After all, this person knows so many important people, and who do we know? This person is practically famous for knowing all these famous people, and what are we famous for? This person travels in exalted circles, and we occasionally make it out to an afternoon matinee because it's five-dollar day at the theater.

Stop right there! Yes, you. Stop comparing yourself to others. Stop looking for your sense of worth in who you know, what you do, or where you go. Instead, look to the Creator of the Universe and see what He says about you.

You are His beloved. Check out the Song of Solomon if you don't believe me.

You are chosen by God, His royal priesthood, a holy nation, sanctified and set apart for His works for you. See 1 Peter 2:9 for confirmation.

You are loved – 2 Thessalonians 2:13.

You are redeemed – Deuteronomy 9:26

And if you still doubt me, read the Psalms – love letters from God to you.

Or look at the price He paid – sending His Son away from Him.

Or the price Jesus paid – crucifixion.

Or the guarantee God has given us that everything He says is true – the Holy Spirit. (Isaiah 63:11)

So the next time somebody tries to make you look or feel inferior, remind them Whose you are.

Takeaway: Don't waste time comparing yourself to others. They aren't the standard.

Exercises:
1. Memorize at least one of the scripture verses referenced above.
2. Journal about your struggle with comparing yourself with others.
3. Pray and ask the Lord to release you from that battle.

Numbers Don't Change

"I prefer numbers to people, because numbers don't change."

I'd made this statement after a particularly hard day at work. I didn't really mean it—at least, not in the global sense of not liking people. I simply didn't much like people that day.

I was trained as an accountant, completing a business degree in college, but my love for numbers started as a child. I counted everything. And if on the second count wasn't the same as the first, I counted again. And if it was the same, I counted again just to confirm once more.

Neurotic, perhaps.

I counted ceiling tiles, floor tiles, cracks in the sidewalk, squares on someone's shirt or tie. I counted people in restaurants, cars in parking lots, birds in flocks.

But if there was one thing I liked more than numbers, it was mysteries. Nancy Drew, Hardy Boys, Bobbsey Twins. And then as I got older, Sherlock Holmes and Agatha Christie. I liked the old-fashioned mysteries where the good guy always wins and the bad guy always get caught.

About ten years ago, I heard about National Novel Writing Month, and I wondered if I had just one book in me. One, that's all I wanted to write.

And since I figured I should write what I know, I decided on a mystery that included an accountant.

Talk about autobiographical.

So I started writing. On November 11th. Already behind. I wrote like a fiend trying to catch up and then to keep up, because I am very competitive, very badge-oriented, and there was a badge to be won when I completed this challenge. Notice I said 'when' and not 'if'.

I had no idea about plotting or character arc. I just wrote a story that had been tumbling around my head for a few years. I got to the last three chapters and had no idea whodunit. So I had to decide that, then go back and put in hints and red herrings, develop some characters a little more to make them suspects, and finish.

There are still days when I prefer numbers over people.

But thankfully, not so many as before.

Takeaway: We all have at least one book in us.

Exercises:
1. What do you love to do? How could you incorporate this into a book idea?
2. Do you have an interesting occupation? Could this become the occupation of your main character?
3. Write out a character sketch of your main character.

One Mouthful at a Time

> GOD, my shepherd!
> I don't need a thing.
> You have bedded me down in lush meadows,
> you find me quiet pools to drink from.
> True to your word,
> you let me catch my breath
> and send me in the right direction.
> (Psalm 23:1-3 The Message)

If you're anything like me, life is rushing past you at supersonic speed, seeming to scatter in all directions like a herd of squirrels. And if you're anything like me, there is no slowing down in the near future. Despite all our technology, we seem to push and stretch to do more with the hours we have, cramming more doing in, despising those moments when we can't do because of a line up or a break down or a need to just be.

And then God reminds us, in poetry meant for our hearts, that He is the One who provides all we need. When we look at the shepherd of King David's day, a lush meadow for him was a rocky hillside where tufts of grass grew in a clump here, a clump there. Seed, watered by the dew and the night fog from the Mediterranean, sprang up overnight and burned off in the hot afternoon sun. If the sheep didn't find it before then, it was gone. And so the shepherd led them across the dry ground to a mouthful of food here, a mouthful there.

And only good shepherds knew where to lead their sheep.

How blessed we are to follow the Great Shepherd, who laid down His life for His sheep. Who tends the flock so that not one is lost. Who sleeps across the gate to the sheepfold so none wander away and the destroyer doesn't get in.

Today, if you are like me, you need a quiet moment to stop, breathe, think, then act.

Take that moment now.
You heard me. Now.
Stop. Breathe. Think. Repeat.
Okay. You can go now.

But plan to come back tomorrow.
God's got a place reserved for you.

Takeaway: God is never too busy for us.

Exercises:
1. Memorize the scripture verses quoted above.
2. Meditate on them today. Ask God to reveal what He would have you learn from these words.
3. Any time you find yourself stressing out, come back to this passage.

The Call to Write

I guess I've always liked to write. I recall in second grade telling my teacher that I wanted to be a writer when I grew up. She told me that to be a good writer, I needed to read a lot. And I did, and still do. As a kid, I'd ride my bicycle to the library on Saturday and get the limit: 10 books. Once I'd read all the books in the children's section that caught my fancy, I wanted to read what was in the adult section (no tweens or YA in those days). But the librarian was concerned. And so she should be. So we arranged that I would choose the books and let her approve them.

As an adult reader who also writes, sometimes I struggled with sitting down at the computer and putting words on the page. I doubted whether anybody wanted to read my stories. I hoped lives would be changed when they read what I wrote, but was I being prideful? Putting too much pressure on myself? Did it have to be perfect? And once written, then what?

As I sat in front of a blank computer screen one day, I did what I should have been doing all along: I prayed. *Lord, help me write what You want me to write.*

And God spoke to my heart: *Let Me dictate the story and you transcribe it.*

That was the answer I needed. No more pressure on me to come up with plot lines or witty dialogue. No more stress about did it have to be perfect or would lives be changed.

Because I came to understand some things about my writing that I've been able to translate into my faith walk:

- God is giving me a brand new story that's never been heard by anybody before. For me.
- So long as He is in control, the story will be perfect. It's only when I get in the way that problems occur.
- Hearing His story has taught me to listen well.
- Knowing this story is first and foremost for me has relieved the stress of who would want to read my stories. I do.
- If I'm not changed by the story, nobody else will be, either. The change must start in me.

Each time I sit to write, I pray: *Lord, please dictate the story and let me transcribe it. Thank you for the opportunity to hear this story for the first time.*

Takeaway: When the story comes from God, it's a story worth telling.

Exercises:
1. Ask the Lord for the stories He wants you to write.
2. Be willing to wait for that story.
3. Despite the fact the Lord gave you the story, don't use that to defend your resistance to editing, critique, and revision.

Am I Invisible?

Do you ever get the feeling that nobody truly sees you for who you are? They only see what you can do for them. Or for how you make them feel.

Sometimes my main character in *A Prickly Affair*, Lily Duncan, feels that way. She's a rough-and-tumble cowgirl in the Arizona Territory, writing romance stories under a pseudonym of Daisy Duncan.

Invisible.

But you aren't.

When people treat us like we don't really count, that can be hurtful, frustrating, demeaning. It can cause us to question our calling, our talents, our very essence.

As the pseudonym for a writer, Daisy only has the calling, the talent, the essence her creator gave her. Notice the use of a small 'c' for creator there.

Lily thinks Daisy is loving, tender, romantic, stylish, and all the things she isn't.

But as a child of God, you have the calling, the talent, the essence your Creator gave you.

Note the capital C.

He says you are beloved, treasured, and all the things He is.

God created us for three things: to worship Him, to fellowship with Him, and to reach out and draw others into His kingdom. All of those purposes work together. Being wholeheartedly invested in one will cause us to grow and overflow into the other purposes.

You are not invisible. You are not the sum of what you do. You are not what others say about you.

You are cradled in the palm of His hand. You are the face of God in a fallen world. You are what He says about you.

So the next time you feel like nobody really sees you, or others overlook who you really are or try to force you into their mold, remember these things:

1. Genesis 21:23 -- You are a foreigner in this world. It isn't our home. It's just the place our physical bodies live while we complete the tasks God has given us.
2. Deuteronomy 7:6 -- You are holy unto God. This means He has sanctified you, He has set you apart for His use. It doesn't matter what others think or say about you.
3. Luke 19:40 -- if we don't fulfill God's call on our lives, He will find someone or something else to do it. We are His hands and feet in this world.

Takeaway: You are important. You are unique. You are called and gifted by God, and nobody--do you hear me?--nobody can say anything different that would be true.

Exercises:
1. Memorize at least one of the scripture verses in the above article so that when the enemy comes to you with a lie, you already have a response for him.
2. Ask the Lord to reveal His next step for you.
3. Be willing to take it.

Touched by an Angel

Hebrews 13:2 (NLT) Don't forget to show hospitality to strangers, for some who have done this have entertained angels without realizing it!

My husband and I belong to a large international ministry that reaches the lost for Christ through Bible distribution. I was recently listening to a testimony by a man who came to know Christ through one of these Bibles. He said, "I don't know where all the other Bibles went, but I know where one went. And some day, in heaven, I'm going to thank that man who gave me the Bible."

No doubt the man who gave this new Christian a Bible doesn't have any idea how this one simple act changed this man, and his family, forever.

In the same way, we don't know how our writing ministry can change lives.

Perhaps, like the man who gave the Bible, you've been writing for a long time and you don't seem to be getting anywhere. Maybe you've been published, but even that didn't make you feel as though you're reaching people. Or, like most of us, perhaps the doors to publication have seemed to slam shut in your face every time you turn around.

In the movie *Julie and Julia*, Julie started out on a project—to create every recipe in Julia Child's first book, and then to blog about it. After a few months, she cried out, in her blog, "Is anybody reading this?"

Is that how you feel about your writing? About your blog? Your Facebook and Twitter posts? That maybe nobody is reading what you write?

Well, there is. How do I know this?

Because I know Who you are writing for.

And He is paying close attention.

As Christians, we must always keep God as our primary audience. Every book, every article, every post, yes, even every devotional, should be written with Him in mind.

When I wrote my father's first memoir, I wanted it to be a book he'd be proud to have his name on.

And then I realized I should also want my Father God to be proud to have His name on every book I write, too.

Only then can we touch lives for Him. Only then can we fulfill the scripture above, entertaining angels with our writing gift.

Lord, please help me to hear Your words and to put them down on paper. Thank You for letting me be the first person to see and hear the story You are showing me. Help me write a story You are proud to put Your name on. In Jesus' name, Amen.

Takeaway: We write for an audience of One first and foremost. The rest are icing on the cake.

Exercises:
1. If you feel you're writing into cyber-space, look for other blogs to guest blog for.
2. Choose a topic of current interest to blog about.
3. Pray and ask for guidance on topics and content.

Subplots that won't sink your story – mini-conference

Regardless of the genre, readers want stories that are more than just surface excursions into the imagination. They want a story worth reading. For your story to make a difference, you must touch your reader at their inner being.

I'm not talking about heart-pounding, scare-the-pants-off-the reader kind of stories, although that could be the kind of book you're writing. Increased heart rate, rising blood pressure, and sob-filled tear-inducing scenes might come to mind, but the truth is, a reader will consider a story worth reading only if it does one thing: makes them think.

For that to happen, you don't need to write a literary masterpiece, or include pages and pages of technical specs, or pen a volume of historical significance—you simply need the reader to ask: would I have done the same thing?

While plots and characters are important to the success of your story, subplots add that layer of color and texture that makes the story even more real. Face it, every genre plot follows the same formula: hero/heroine wants something they can't have, and you, as the author, have to work out the details so that they either get what they want or they figure out they don't really want that thing but they want something else instead.

And this is where subplots come in. Subplots are the explanation for why the character wants what they want and why they can't have it, and subplots also explain why they change their mind later on or what resolve they garner that propels them on to the conclusion.

Let's look at some definitions first, so we're all on the same page.

<u>Plot</u>: it's what's going on in the story. From the part where you start, "it's a story about" until you end with "and that's the end of the story", plot is the middle part, like the filling in an Oreo cookie.

And just like the filling in a vanilla Oreo is different than the filling in a mint Oreo, the plot of your story is going to be different than the plot of anybody else's story, simply because you're going to combine the ingredients differently.

The purpose of the plot is to highlight the strengths and weaknesses of your characters; to give them a chance to grow and change, or to make decisions not to grow and change.

Characters: it's the people in the story. A main character is WHO the story is about, and secondary characters are like a supporting cast. You need people apart from the main characters because we all have people in our lives apart from our main characters.

For example, in my household, there is my husband and me. We would be the main characters in our story. But from time to time, I need to introduce and show our three housemates, because they live in the same house, we interact with them, they sometimes cause tension in our relationship, and they cause tension between themselves.

Theme: This is the overarching reason you're writing the story. No, we're not looking for some grandiose statement like "the story is about spiritual warfare". Face it, as Christians, all of our books should be about spiritual warfare. But spiritual warfare in what context? So maybe your book is about a crooked cop who has to make different moral choices if he wants a different outcome. That is the theme of my historical novel, *Counterfeit Honor*. Or the theme of my cozy mysteries, written under my pen name, Leeann Betts, is that God gives us second. . . and third. . . and fourth chances.

Subplots: You can create layers of plots much like you layer a lasagna—you start with the bottom layer, which is your main plot, and then you add the ingredients of the smaller stories called subplots. Just like a good lasagna—where one layer would be boring and not satisfying but twenty layers would be overwhelming—you choose how many subplots to include. We'll talk more about that next week, figuring out how many subplots to include.

A good subplot could stand alone as its own story, IF it weren't trying to exist in the shadow of the main plot line. However, a good subplot needs characters—usually most of the same characters as the main plot, although it is perfectly okay to have one or two characters that appear only in the context of the subplot. A good subplot needs a reason to be there, not simply because you wanted to tell two stories at the same time. A really good subplot introduces tensions into the main plot that wouldn't be there if the subplot wasn't there, and if the subplot can add reasons as to why the main characters are being hindered from achieving their goal, so much the better.

Layering: You can choose to have one main plot and nothing else. We find that a lot in what is called Category Romance. This is the boy-meets-girl boy-loses-girl boy-gets-girl romances, often books of 60,000 words or less, that you might buy at the supermarket checkout or receive monthly through a book club. They are straight romance with all of the tension and problems originating within the relationship, and all of the solutions tying themselves up neatly through the relationship. These books usually have about four main characters: heroine, hero, heroine's best friend, and another love interest that tries to keep the heroine and hero apart. There are minimal secondary characters, often an employer or an employee, a neighbor, a neighborhood acquaintance, but these are limited because this kind of plot focuses on getting the hero and heroine together quickly, which means they have to spend a lot of time together.

Your book might have the main plot and one subplot. Novellas, even as short as 20,000 words, are often structured this way. For example, in my recent novella release, "Echoes of the Heart", in the *Pony Express Romance Collection*, the main plot line is the romance—or potential romance—between my hero and heroine. The subplot is a mysterious woman who travels the Pony Express under various assumed names and steals from men she befriends. While this may seem completely unrelated to my main plot, consider this: my heroine is living under the assumed name of her best friend who has died. When this comes to light, you can see how my hero quickly jumps to the wrong conclusion about my heroine's true identity.

Different genres require differing levels of complexity and thus increasing numbers of subplots. For example, a psychological thriller might have the main plot and three to four subplots. In a mystery, the subplots often tie into the main plot. In epic works such as family sagas, there could be four or more subplots in each volume, only one or two of which are tied up by the end of that volume, with the remaining plots carrying over into the next.

Pivot Points are those places where your plot has been going along for a little while, and you work in a circumstance, situation, or reaction that takes the plot in a seemingly different direction. However, you need to be careful with how you use this because your plot is defined by your genre to a large extent, so that new direction must still be in accordance with your genre. For example, if you're writing a category romance and you decide to throw in a murder mystery, while that may take the story in a different direction, it isn't what the reader expects. And while it's good to surprise readers, we don't want them to stop reading. We want them to say, "oh, that's good. I didn't see that coming".

Exercise
So think about your own work in process. What genre are you writing in? How many main characters do you have? Do you see, from this lesson, where you might make some changes?

Write a one-sentence summary of the plot and each subplot(s) of your current work in process. So if you have two subplots, you should have three sentences.

For example, in my recent release, *Echoes of the Heart,* I have the main plot and one subplot:
A stationmaster in Utah needs help, and a young woman in Boston needs a fresh start.

When the young woman assumes her dead friend's identity and travels to Utah to get married, she doesn't know there is a criminal traveling the route who seduces men and then robs them.

Think about your current work in process. If you're not writing right now, don't worry. We'll help you brainstorm through the plot and subplots necessary to make your book memorable. So if you haven't done the previous assignments, do them now. They provide the groundwork for moving forward.

So now that we've spent some time learning the terminology and practiced summarizing our plot and subplots, let's turn to talking about layers.

Layering is the term we use when we weave the plot and subplots into one cohesive unit. If we don't weave the different plot layers together, what we tend to end up with are disparate stories that touch each other through only one point, such as a character or the setting. However, layered plot lines are as difficult to untangle as a bowl of spaghetti, such that the reader knows that even when they're spending time in one plot line, the other plot lines continue, progress, and get more complicated.

When layering is done correctly, you will never go back in time in your story. So, for example, if your scene for plot line 1 ends with Sally and Tom driving down a dark road after dinner on their way home which normally takes them ten minutes, and the next scene covers about three hours in plot line 2 where Joan and Brick get into a huge argument after spending two hours painting a room, when you return to plot line 1, you'd better be three hours along in time. This means that Sally and Tom aren't just arriving home, unless you give a good reason, such as they got lost, they had a flat tire, or they pulled over to talk. Otherwise, you've just separated your layers and probably lost your reader.

So, as promised, we're going to talk a little about word count. When you set out to write your story, you need to know how long the story should be because: (a) you need to tell the story completely, and (b) you need to know what the market expects. A basic single-plot story, such as a category romance, will run up to about 50,000 words. Any more than that, and the reader is going to get bored.

To increase the word count, you add plot lines. One plot line adds about 10,000 words. Two will add another 10,000, and so on. More than three subplots can get confusing, so if you still need to add words, rather than ramble on and on about nothing, which again is something readers don't like, and rather than add in yet another subplot, you might consider adding in another main character, which will also add about another 10,000 words. So in a romantic suspense of 80,000 words, you'd have the main plot line, two subplots, and three main characters.

Likewise, if you need to cut words from your manuscript, you might consider whether you have too many subplots or main characters.

Let's say you find your word count is too high—where do you start cutting? Consider whether you might have two characters serve a dual purpose. For example, let's say you need a firefighter and a best friend for the hero. Make the hero's best friend a firefighter.

You might also think about having one scene serve a dual purpose. So if you need to reveal that the heroine was bullied in school and so is afraid of overpowering men, and you also need to have something come between the hero and heroine to keep them apart a little longer, you might have the hero listen to his friend who tells him that in order to win his girl's heart, he needs to step in and be forceful, and when he does, she sees a bully and reveals this part of her backstory or her wound in internal dialogue.

<u>Backstory</u> is the part of your character's life that happened before the story began. While it's important for the reader to know what motivates your character, what has shaped your character's life so they understand why your character makes the choices they make, it can also seem like an information dump that yanks the story to a halt.

Instead of telling the reader everything you know about your character, intimate their past. Allude to their wound or the lie they believe. Have them wonder if they'll ever get over whatever it is, but don't come right out and say something like, "Maggie was bullied in school and so cannot stand men who raise their voice at her, so when Greg shouted, she didn't like that and felt threatened by him."

Instead, you might say something like: Maggie sighed. Men are the same everywhere, whether they're in the school yard or on the school board.

From this, we know there is something that happened to Maggie in school, and that is the lie she believes and that shapes her choices.

Subplots serve another important job, and that is to give the readers a break from the main action. So if there has been a tension-intensive chapter or two, this might be a good place to weave in a small subplot so the reader gets a chance to sit back and take a deep breath. By its very nature, a subplot will be less intense than the main plotline.

Subplots can also help repair the dreaded Middle Muddle. This part of your story can occur when you're just going on day to day, working toward the end of the story with the gunfight or the car chase, but not a lot is happening. If you are bored writing the story at this point, the reader will also be bored. Introduce a new subplot to occupy the characters, increase tension, show another side of their life, and erase the boredom.

Hopefully I've given you some food for thought about your current work in process. Maybe you've even thought of some ways to make changes to your story.

Exercise First of all, take a look at the plot and subplot summary you did earlier. Now I want you to think about the last lesson and ask yourself some questions:

- Do you need to increase or decrease your word count? If so, consider adding or reducing plot lines or characters.
- Can you make any of your characters or scenes serve two purposes?
- Is there a Middle Muddle in your story? Add a new subplot.

Now go back to your original summary and make whatever changes you think you need to incorporate these revisions. Which one do you think tells your story more fully?

Keeping your subplots under control.
We're all writers here, and we know the excitement of starting a new project. Sometimes we don't want to take the time to plot out the story, or create character profiles for even our main characters. In fact, I admit it, sometimes I take the first two or three chapters just getting to know my characters. Then I junk most of it and write some fresh stuff to get the story going again.

However, if you don't take the time to at least know where the story is going—even if you know in your head but don't commit it to paper—you're going to end up writing either a very long convoluted story, or you'll write yourself into a corner and end up having to fix it later.

Some writers think that knowing where the story goes limits the creativity. I say it does quite the opposite. When I sit down to write a book, I know where the story starts and where it's going to end up. The middle part is often a bit cloudy for me, which is like seeing gifts wrapped under the Christmas tree. I know there is something good there with my name on it, but I don't know what it is right now. That's the joy of discovering the middle of the book.

So I've said all that to encourage you to write out your plot summary and your subplot summaries. These sentences will serve two purposes: (a) to keep you on track when your characters want to take you down yet another rabbit trail, and (b) to remind you of what a great story you have when it comes to the middle muddle, that time when most writing projects are abandoned.

As I said, I'm a writer, and I love it when a character shows me something unexpected, or says something that I hadn't planned. I know the character is alive in my head when that happens, and when they are alive in my head, it's my job to make them alive to my readers. These revelations are not limited by your plot summaries. In fact, they should enhance the summary since you should discover that although surprising, the revelation isn't out of character.

But when a character tries to take us in another direction than the plot summaries, we must seriously consider whether we have a completely different story in mind, or whether perhaps this is a diversion we need to ignore. Let's take the story of *Cinderella*, for example. We're going along with the opening scenes where the wicked stepmother and stepsisters are taking advantage of Cinderella. She's dreaming of her Prince Charming coming along and rescuing her. And then she gets a letter in the mail, and she's offered a full scholarship to Wonderland University to pursue a law degree and—wait a minute. That's not in the plot summaries. That's not in the story. And if she'd decided to go to law school, that would be a completely different story. So you can see that checking the new story line against your plot summaries helps keeps you on track.

If this new plot line absolutely won't leave you alone, what do you do? Again, one of two things (are you seeing a pattern here?) (a) you can toss it out—actually, make a note of it and keep it in a file for another story, or (b) change your initial plot summary to include this new line of thought, and save the original for a different story.

Exercise: So far you've thought about your story, its plot summaries, its subplots, characters, and scenes. Now what I want you to do is to add one more subplot to your original story. I realize this step might increase your word count beyond what is normal for your genre and market, but bear with me.

Pick or create a subplot that comes from a main character's backstory.

So, for example, as I showed before, let's use Maggie and Greg. We know Maggie was bullied in school and so is leery of forceful men. You might add a subplot that has Maggie falling in love with the boy who bullied her, only she doesn't know it's him. But he recognizes Maggie, and he is out to make her life a living hell. He is on his best behavior, so she doesn't see what's going on. But Greg does. And when he tells Maggie, she won't believe him because she thinks Greg just doesn't want her to be happy. And when she won't listen to him, Greg starts shouting at her to wake up and see what's going on.

In this example, you can see how the new subplot will layer in with the existing plot layers. Maggie doesn't want anything to do with Greg because he scares her. Maggie still believes the lie and suffers from the wound of her past. All of this feeds into the relationship between Greg and Maggie, and this guy's weird treatment of Maggie could feed into the suspense plot when Maggie goes missing and Greg is certain this guy is responsible. Only he isn't. Somebody else is, but Greg spends all his time trying to prove the bully took her, which means the real culprit is not being pursued.

Exercise: Rewrite the first scene of your work in process from the point of view of this new subplot character from the backstory. Don't just change the names—get into your new subplot character's head. In the example I gave, Harold (the schoolyard bully and now new beau) has a backstory too—don't they all?—he was abused by his father, and nobody ever saved him, so when he could, he left home, changed his name, but hasn't changed his behavior.

Then answer the following questions about this new scene:
Will your new POV change the story completely?
Which version do you like better? Why?

In my example, I don't see it changing the story completely, but it has added another layer to Maggie's character, that she would fall for the same guy or same kind of guy twice. When she finds out, will she be convinced she can't be trusted to choose the right kind of guy? Or will she learn from her mistake and move on. Will Greg figure out he can't push his way through a problem, despite what his mother taught him about nose to the grindstone and all that? And will Harold decide to change his behavior and not hold everybody else responsible for his father's mistakes and his own bad choices? I would include this new revelation to deepen the tension and conflict.

Dreaming up Drama. As you sit down to work on your current manuscript or on future pieces, you're going to need some ideas, a.k.a. plot lines, to keep the story moving. As we've seen in this course, even if you want to tell a simple love story, your characters have other things going on in their lives besides the romance, even if sometimes it might feel that the romance is the only important event at the moment.

So where do we find additional great plot lines, a.k.a. story ideas?

- Look to real life: listen to the news; read the paper; check online news sources; read biographies. Don't limit yourself to the words—look at the pictures. One of my favorite books that I wrote, *Counterfeit Honor*, came from a picture in a newspaper celebrating the 50th anniversary of the shooting of Lee Harvey Oswald. There was a picture of the detective who was escorting Oswald to court, and Jack Ruby in the foreground, his gun drawn. The detective said he told Oswald, just before they stepped into that area, that he hoped that anybody gunning for Oswald was as good a shot as Oswald was, meaning he hoped they would hit Oswald and not him. I saw that picture and wondered what it would be like if the detective knew someone was going to kill Oswald, and the story grew from there.

- Look to the lives of your main characters: is there something in their occupation, their family lives, their hobbies, that might provide an additional plot line? For example, in my cozy mystery series featuring Carly Turnquist, her husband is a computer programmer, which has provided me with many locations where he goes to do his contract work and Carly tags along and ultimately gets herself into trouble.

- Consider what will keep your characters from achieving their goal. For example, if your character's goal is to win a medal at the local track meet, what might prevent that? An injury? If so, was it accidental or deliberate? A failed exam gets her kicked off the high school team? What if she paid for the answers but didn't get the right cheat sheet? Perhaps her car broke down on the way to the meet—again, accident or deliberate? The answers to all these questions will open doors for the next step in the story, and may even suggest additional plot lines. For example, if her car was tampered with, perhaps by the hero because he doesn't want her to win because he knows if she does, she'll go on to nationals and he'll be left behind because he isn't as good an athlete as she is.

Resources

There are many great online resources and books available regarding writing, too numerous to mention all of them here. However, I will include a list of resources that have helped me.

Writing groups:

American Christian Fiction Writers: www.acfw.com . ACFW has local chapters in most states, and offers online critique groups, online courses, and savings when registering for their conference.

Sisters in Crime: for sisters and brothers who write suspense, mystery, thriller, police or legal procedurals -- www.SistersInCrime.org . SinC has local chapters in many state and offers a discount at conferences for members.

Romance Writers of America: www.rwa .

Research:

Wikipedia: search for "list of museums in (state)"

Your local librarian -- they love to help with research

Chamber of Commerce

Historical Society -- many towns have a historical society with docents who love to talk about the history.

Conferences:

American Christian Fiction Writers: annual conference that moves around the country -- www.acfw.com/conference

Sisters in Crime: annual conference that moves around the country, as well as regional conferences -- www.SisterInCrime.org/?page=13

Killer Nashville: annual conference in Nashville, Tennessee that features forensics, crime, psychology, and more -- www.KillerNashville.com

Colorado Christian Writers Conference: annual conference held in Estes Park, Colorado – http://Colorado.WriteHisAnswer.com

Romance Writers of America: annual conference that moves around the country -- www.rwa.org

Philadelphia Christian Writers Conference: annual conference held in Philadelphia, PA – http://Philadelphia.WriteHisAnswer.com

Mount Hermon Christian Writers Conference: annual conference held in Mt. Hermon, CA – http://Writers.MountHermon.org

Shaw Guides to Writers Conferences and Workshops: a great place to see if there is a conference or workshop happening some place you're traveling to or through: http://writing.shawguides.com

Online learning opportunities:

www.FutureLearn.com -- offers free university-quality courses that you can do at your own pace; check out Identifying the Dead, a course on forensics that takes you through a mock crime scenario, or 100 Stories, a Word War 1 course that introduces you to 100 men and women from Australia and New Zealand and the impact of the war on their lives.

www.WritersDigest.com -- offers many courses specifically for writers; usually a cost associated with these courses

Most writers groups offer online courses, including ACFW, which are free to members

www.ChristianPen.com -- offers courses for editors and proofreaders that usually have a nominal cost

About the Author (s)

Donna Schlachter and her alter ego, Leeann Betts, write from Denver, Colorado. Donna/Leeann is married with two adult daughters and 11 grandchildren. She is also attended by two cats of gigantic proportions, Samson and Gideon.

Donna pens historical suspense/romance while Leeann focuses on contemporary suspense and cozy mysteries. They are hybrid authors who have published a number of books with many more in the words. They are a member of American Christian Fiction Writers and Sisters In Crime; they facilitate a local critique group, and they teach writing classes and courses. Donna is also a ghostwriter and editor of fiction and non-fiction, and judges in a number of writing contests. She loves history and research, and travels extensively for both, while Leeann is 'cute and perky and everything Donna isn't'. They are proud to be represented by Terrie Wolf of AKA Literary Management.

Donna blog: www.HiStoryThruTheAges.wordpress.com
Donna website and newsletter: www.HiStoryThruTheAges.com Receive a free ebook simply for signing up for our free newsletter!
Leeann blog: www.AllBettsAreOff.wordpress.com
Leeann website and newsletter: www.LeeannBetts.com Receive a free ebook just for signing up for our quarterly newsletter.
Donna Facebook: www.Facebook.com/DonnaschlachterAuthor
Leeann Facebook: http://bit.ly/1pQSOqV
Donna Twitter: www.Twitter.com/DonnaSchlachter
Leeann Twitter: http://bit.ly/1qmqvB6
Donna Books: Amazon: http://amzn.to/2ci5Xqq and
Donna Smashwords: http://bit.ly/2gZATjm
Leeann Books: Amazon http://amzn.to/2dHfgCE and Leeann Smashwords: http://bit.ly/2z5ecP8